ECONOMIC REFORMS AND VITAL SECTORS OF INDIA

ECONOMIC REFORMS
and
VITAL SECTORS OF INDIA

BROJENDRA NATH BANERJEE

GYAN PUBLISHING HOUSE
NEW DELHI-110 002

ISBN : 81-212-0431-3

Published in 1993 by
Gyan Publishing House, 5, Ansari Road
Delhi - 110002

Composed by Sita Computers, Delhi, and printed at Goyal
Offset Works, Delhi

DEDICATION

JYOTI AND NADINE

"No-one lights a lamp and puts it in a place where it will be hidden, or under a bowl. Instead he puts it on its stand, so that those who come in may see the light.

"Your eye is the lamp of your body, when your eyes are good, your whole body also is full of light...."

St. Luke 11:33-34

INTRODUCTION

One of the best documents suggesting well considered remedies on the present economic crises comes from the four economists, namely, Prof. P. N. Dhar, Dr. I. G. Patel, Shri M. Narsimhan and Shri R.N. Malhotra. The present government seemed to be following their advice to a large extent. That it was coming up simultaneously with the devaluation of the rupee, with a package of the economic reforms was clear from the new trade reforms policy announced by the government.

The issue which suddenly came up in the forefront was the extreme haste with which the Rao government ordered two instalments of devaluation of the rupee, one after another within a short span of four days reducing the rupee value by almost 20 per cent, which was probably what was far more than resorted to during Indira Gandhi's regime in 1966. This threw the economy totally out of gear - though the devaluation was said to aim only at saving an acute foreign exchange crisis.

The step - announced by the Reserve Bank of India (RBI)— as a backdoor devaluation now seemed to cover extensive sectors in the economy, and India would have to introduce a whole host of economic measures in order to secure around US $ 7 billion worth of foreign exchange loan from the International Monetary Fund (IMF). The opposition parties were bitter in their condemnation of the measure taken by the Congress minority government under the Premiership of P.V. Narasimha Rao and called it all "sell out" to American pressure. The devaluation of the rupee was a thorny issue. Why was it adopted in such haste, with the session of the Parliament only four days away, was being questioned by all political parties.

The implications of the devaluation are manifold: To start with, by rendering imports more expensive, it is inflationary. This would be so even if the government does not raise administrative prices of goods like oil which it imports. But that would mean an additional burden of expenditure on the government in a period when there is general agreement that the fiscal deficit should be cut. Further, the rupee cost of servicing external debt will rise in proportion to the depreciation aggravating the fiscal crisis.

So the net effect of devaluation will be high inflation, worsening fiscal problems, greater recession, or a combination of these. Since the responsiveness of exports to steady real devaluations of the 1980s has not been remarkable, it is not clear that the costs of this devaluation will be compensated by widening exports, especially since export subsidies are to be reduced even as costs of production increase.

Devaluation or depreciation of the rupee was not an end in itself. It was the means of an end. But the question was not whether devaluation was good or bad for the economy from the IMF's point of view. It was whether those who were managing India's economic crisis believed it was the correct step to take. One was aware that the black market rates for the U.S. dollar were around Rs. 27 when the official price was around Rs. 21 and that the black market rate was considered a fairer indication of the rupee's value than the official rate. But one was also aware that devaluation would be fraught with grave consequences especially on the price front.

Consequent to the historic measures of restructuring the country's economy and also its currency exchange rates, the Indian rupee recorded an all-time fall against all major world currencies during the year 1991 thanks to the Reserve Bank of India's move to depreciate the currency by a cumulative 20 per cent on two successive occasions on July 1 and 3, 1991. In spite of the Reserve Bank's efforts to keep the rupee stable against the U.S. dollar, the rupee fell steeply by approximately 43 per cent against the dollar at Rs. 25.85.38 per cent against the British pound at Rs 47.50, 37 per cent against the Deutschemark at Rs 16.60 and about 34 per cent against the Yen at Yen 497 per Rs. 100. Clarifying the slump, a top-ranking RBI official said that this was "inevitable" because of the downward adjustment in the value of the rupee against the basket of currencies in terms of the pound sterling which had appreciated against the US dollar in the recent past..... Providing statistics for the second half period of the year, the official said that the U.S. dollar depreciated to the extent of more than 12 per cent against the pound over the level of July 3 while the rupee's depreciation against the pound was only 11.86 per cent. In fact, the rupee appreciated by 0.26 per cent against the dollar during the same period.

At the parity's level, the rupee was adjusted about 163 times downwards and 124 upwards during the year, resulting in a sharp fall of 30 to 45 per cent against all major currencies in the world. Finding clues from the fact that the Indian currency was over-valued against major world currencies, RBI devalued the rupee by 8.76 per cent and 11.83 per cent respectively on July 1 and 3 bringing a total fall of about Rs. 7.50 in the rupee value in just 48 hours. Earlier, during the first half of the year ending June 28, the rupee was down by 16.5 per cent against the dollar and 12.4 per cent against the yen. But it posted gains by about 4 per cent against the Deutschemark and 2 per cent against the British pound during the same period. At the same time, the dollar rose by 17 per cent against the pound and 22 per cent against the Mark in overseas centres.

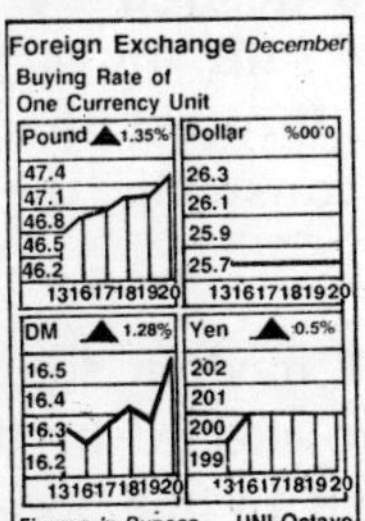

Came July and the sudden depreciation of the rupee by about 20 per cent which had led to chaos and confusion in Indian foreign exchange markets with increased withdrawal of funds from India by investors, particularly the non-resident Indians (NRIs). Sensing the adverse impact it might have on the overall economy RBI clarified that in the five month period between February and June 1991, the nominal effective exchange rate declined only by 2.5 per cent. Therefore, there was a need for an adjustment in the exchange rate as the country's competitiveness in exports was being eroded. Since October last year (1990) there was actually some appreciation of about two per cent in the effective real exchange rate due to slower rate of depreciation and widening inflation differentials. Reacting to the rupee's sharp fall during the year, foreign bankers said this would be a continuous process since the rupee, which is to be made a convertible currency, would have to be adjusted regularly for inflation differentials which scaled to a peak of about 16 per cent during the year.

Inspite of RBI's repeated assurance that the rupee would not be further devalued, it was noticed that the fall of the currency was at the much higher side during the year in contrast to the US dollar's gain of 3 per cent against the pound and 4.5 per cent against the Deutschemark. In fact, the possibility of the US economy recovering in the coming year is bleak following an expected fall in industrial production, farm production and a subsequent cut in interest rate. In that case, there is every possibility of a weak dollar in the coming months and subsequently, the Indian currency would have to adjusted downward in order to keep it stable against the dollar, as desired by the Central monetary authority -RBI - they said. In fact, an investment company in Hong Kong, forecast that a weak US economy would continue to constrain the dollar while yen is seen strengthening.

Every institution of modern society and every aspect of individual life styles are affected by the availability of energy in its various forms and by the social costs involved in the production and use of that energy. Industrial production is patterned on cheap motive and thermal energy. Residential and urban patterns are shaped by the availability of cheap liquid fuels. Modern life-styles depend on transportation at the turn of the ignition key and on electrical energy at the flick of a switch.

Estimated World Energy Stocks

Type	Reserves	(10^{15} Btu Resources)	Years to exhaustion (from 1975) at Current Rates	Years to exhaustion (from 2050) at 2050 Use Rates
Crude Oil	4,000	12,000	100	25
Natural Gas	2,000	10,000	200	100
Coal	6,000	200,000	3,000	170
Heavy Oil	2,000	20,000	500*	200
Stall Oil	2,000	12,000	300*	200
Tur Sands	200	6,000	150*	100
Uranium	1,000	2,000	600	0

Sources: World Energy Outlook, SRI International, estimates in CEQ, Global 2000 Study, P. 111, are somewhat lower
*. After depletion of conventional oil stocks.

We can reduce consumption of energy but we can not eliminate it. It is energy that fuels the GNP, and if we do not have enough even with our best conservation efforts, there will be serious economic consequences. Increasing energy prices to their present levels have significantly affected the economy. At some point we will need an energy price ceiling to prc'ect the economy from decline. GNP influences energy demand much more than energy availability influences GNP.

A few words about Fusion Energy

The concept is simple and proven. With the proper conditions of temperature and pressure one can fuse together rare forms of hydrogen (denterium and tritium) and create and release large amounts of energy. This process has been demonstrated in thermonuclear explosions, but to apply the process to commercial power generation requires a very different technology. The industry has been working on the problem for a long time now, but achieving controlled fusion has proved to be harder than expected. Research scientists are still waiting for the net energy breakthrough, when more energy is obtained from the reaction than was used to create it.

It is finally beginning to look as though that point may be near. About a dozen teams of researchers, using different kinds of machine, have been making steady progress in recent years, both in the inertial and magnetic confinement approaches. There is now an air of expectation, and during the next five years exciting announcements to the effect that they have surpassed the breakeven point may be forthcoming.

Granted these scientific breakthroughs, a critical question is how practical fusion will be as a means of generating electrical power. The process will have to involve not only the scientific laboratories but also teams of people who have successfully engineered practical fission reactors, and so a lot of engineering remains to be done after the scientists have shown that it works. A number of preliminary concepts have already been developed. A lot of hard work, good luck and money will be needed before we start feeding fusion power into our electrical grids (see appendix).

There is reason for optimism regarding our energy future. First, we must get to the year 2000, however, without intervening, economic problems that can keep us from pushing hard on all the technologies that offer promise to deliver major amounts of energy in the near term, the medium term, and the long term. That requires action now.

In recent years we have experienced a period of more or less public disenchantment with technology as a way of solving our problems. Without an aggressive technological effort there is little hope for an era of plentiful energy. With such an effort we cannot only provide plentiful energy, but in the process of properly applying science and technology to one of our most pressing needs. We can also help to restore public confidence in science and technology and provide for a better life.

A Grave Economic Crisis

In the fiscal year about to end, which has, according to the media, ushered in a glorious era of economic rejuvenation, both agricultural and industrial production have lagged behind the previous year's output, unemployment has increased by a few millions and inflation has reached unprecedented heights. Given our total indebtedness which now touches $ 75 billion, that is more than Rs. 200,000 crore, the outstanding problem is of servicing this indebtedness, which will amount to at least Rs. 15,000 crore annually on the average and, in some individual years, even rise to Rs. 20,000 crore. Today we are a bankrupt nation. The Indian Government's liabilities exceed its assets by Rs. 24,000 crore. All this happened swiftly between 1980 and now. For 10 years from 1980, the carpenters, masons and other traditional Indian hands had pumped $ 26 billion into India from the Gulf countries. This is over six times the IMF loan. This is more than the foreign currency the modern large industries of the Tatas, Birlas, Ambanis and others could earn for India in 40 years. A further $ 16 billion came by way of deposits from non-resident Indians. This collateral input of $ 42 billion alone saved India through the 80s and not the IMF.

The Indian consumers save over 23 per cent of their income even though they spend 70 per cent of it on food and housing. To reduce the imports and to make exports profitable, the finance minister devalued the rupee by more than 20 per cent. In the process, more than 20 million tonnes of import of crude oil and petroleum products from the Gulf countries became more costly. It is estimated that within a year the import bill of these items will go up by Rs. 3,000 crore. With this excessive rise, the government will be forced to increase the prices of petroleum products like diesel, kerosene and petrol by a substantial amount and it will cause an unavoidable rise in the prices of essential commodities.

Let there be no mistake that it was not only the high priced rupee that was responsible for India's tardy export growth. Had it been so, exports would have responded to the steady erosion of the rupee value. In 1990, there was an approximate depreciation of 25 per cent in the value of the rupee. This was accompanied by a six per cent rise in exports—on a small base to begin with—while imports shot up by 13 per cent on a larger base. This revealed that devaluation export link was suspect that would help it establish this calculation even in the long run. Not that an export-led growth was beyond India's capabilities.

According to experts, an adequate emphasis must be given to the production in infrastructure areas - ports steel, metal and power - on which other industrial growth and employment depends. The growth in the sector of power generation has been much lower compared even to that of other developing countries in the world. In the absence of adequate power supply, not more than 40 per cent of the installed capacity of our industry could be used. India has been virtually stagnating at a production level between 10 to 12 million tonnes of steel for nearly 15 to 20 years. In spite of heavy investment in the public sector which exceeds Rs. 100,000 crore, there is no chance of a much quicker augmentation of productivity in the industrial sector in the absence of sufficient power generation.

What we should be concerned with is accelerated and efficient development of power generation, in particular. In this matter, there can be no compromise because stagnation in power generation will not only increase the cost but will have an adverse effect on production of all other sectors in the economy. It is well known that electricity is a basic need, both for agricultural production, particularly in the field of irrigation for tapping underground water resources, and also for production of industrial goods and services. Compared to any developed country in the world, the per capita availability of power, in spite of commendable efforts in improving the installed capacity, is far below the world standard; when we consider the fact that we are hardly near 200 Kwtt per capita as compared to more than 1,000 Kwtt per capita for even some of the developing countries and about 7,000 Kwtt in the developed world.

But when we consider the fact that the generation of power in India is now becoming one of the costliest in the world and consider the purchasing power within the country based on per capita income, it will be seen that any increase of the cost of the new units as well as increase in the cost of raw materials like natural gas and coal, will further shoot up the price of electricity, adversely affecting the cost of production of all other goods and services, including agricultural produce. "We shall be caught in a vicious circle from which it will then become difficult to extricate ourselves", says an expert.

Here again, the only answer is accelerated growth in the generation of power irrespecative of whether it is in the so-called private and public sectors. Natural gas can provide the best and the quickest resource for increasing power generation. It is essential that the cost of new units, which is likely to go up due to devaluation, is maintained by reducing the customs duty so that in the long run the project costs do not go out of control in order to produce power at a higher cost.

Vasant Sathe, the former Union Minister for Energy concludes:[1] "The moment this nation shows a collective will, utilises its vast untapped resources in the parallel economy, releases the energy for increased production, productivity and international competitiveness, encourage the NRIs in particular and the international investors in general, to come and utilise the rich natural resources and skilled man power in India itself, we will find a dramatic change in the entire economic scene and the country may not then be required to seek assistance from IMF or such other sources".

Brojendra Nath Banerjee

C-17 Nizamuddin West
New Delhi-110 013.

1. The Hindustan Times, July 14, 1991.

Chapter I

Vital Sectors of the Economy

Too many far-reaching developments have taken place at too fast a pace on paper, at least. The real issue is what the government is going to do about the real economic problems. One of the assumptions about the present economic crisis has been that the problem is only with the financial sector, and that in purely physical terms the economy is in reasonably fine fettle. The facts and figures presented in the Economic Survey 1990-91 must force some reconsideration of this conclusion. For while over-all economic growth is estimated to be a healthy 5 per cent, the sectoral figures need to be seen in perspective. Thus, the growth of electricity generation for 1990-91 was the lowest in eight years, only twice in the past decade has industry grown slower than it did during 1990-91, and the rise in wholesale price has been the greatest in a decade - despite a slowing down the growth of money supply. That's (in percentage terms) for only the second time in the past decade. Perhaps the one sector that has propped up the rest of the economy has been agriculture.

Two sectors have become problem areas : Energy and infrastructure. In energy, oil production has been short of target and will be so again for the current year (1991-92). There has been a problem with domestic oil production partly due to the Assam agitation. Coal production has faced clear problems and already the growth of power generation in 1990-91 was the slowest in eight years. With a poor performance being notable in the thermal power plants, even refinery production of crude throughout declined by 0.3 per cent during 1990-91 compared to an increase of 6.9 per cent during 1989-90. As per the latest information available non-commercial energy (fuel wood, agricultural and animal waste, wind and solar power) constitutes about 40 per cent of our energy supply while commercial energy constitutes the rest. Within the commercial energy sector hydro-electric power constitutes only

3 per cent, nuclear power supplies only 1 per cent, coal and lignites supplies 56 per cent and oil and natural gas about 40 per cent.

As regards the end use of petroleum products, the household sector consumes about 20 per cent of petroleum products, mainly as a fuel for domestic cooking and lighting. The transport sector consumes about 48 per cent of petroleum products as fuel for vehicles, tractors, airlines, shipping and defence. The industrial sector consumes about 32 per cent of petroleum products as feed stocks or fuel for fertilisers, petrochemicals, agricultural pump sets, thermal power plants, road construction and a variety of industrial applications.

India depends on imports of oil to a large extent to meet its domestic consumption of petroleum products presently estimated at about 54 million tonnes. The cost of oil imports in 1990-91 which was projected at Rs. 6,400 crore in April 1990, is now estimated around Rs. 10,800 crore due to a sharp increase in international prices of oil caused by the Gulf crisis in 1990. Within the power sector, the performance of both the thermal and nuclear sectors is poor while hydro- electricity generation exceeded the targets. The average load factor in the thermal sector at 53.8 per cent during 1990-91 was lower compared with 56.5 per cent during 1989-90.

Load Shedding

Load shedding has become a common feature in everyday life of our cities. In summer, it frequents more than at other times. Every citizen of Calcutta metropolis will never forget July 2, 1991. It was the worst day of power cuts. No train moved out of Howrah and Sealdah Stations that day. All India Radio and Doordarshan shut down. Water supply was badly hit. Office attendance dipped. A part of Calcutta University closed shop. But few of the city people were livid. Even angry. Ask them why. And they said, oh, but this is Calcutta. A regular feature of daily life. Ten years ago in 1981, Bombay also plunged into darkness...for all of seven minutes. This made the headline the next day in the newspapers. Crazy? Ah, that was Bombay. In fact, no city had been spared of power cuts. Delhi Electric Supply Undertaking (DESU) has similar stories to tell. And at times it is worse than those of Calcutta and Bombay. For hours over summer months there is no electricity. Delhi is eternally condemned to darkness. If this is the condition at the seat of authority, how could anybody expect anything better anywhere in India? India has virtually entered into a history of permanent load shedding.

Three years ago, the Goenkas of CEAT fame, got hold of about 20 per cent of Calcutta Electric Supply Corporation (CESC) shares. CESC was always a private limited Company, but this was the first time a big industrial house had such a large stake in it. The Goenkas had pulled off one of the quietest coups in corporate history - and not without the tacit support of the ruling Left Front Government. It was felt that with the advent of the Goenkas, the power situation would improve.

DESU is Corrupt !

A suicide note exposes DESU's corruption. Shri Mritunjay Upadhyaya an Electrical Inspector of Delhi Electric Supply Undertaking committed suicide because an Assistant Engineer (AE) used to instruct Mr. Mritunjay that he should give him Rs. 1000.00 every day because this has been the practice at DESU office in the past also.

"In the very first week of his joining on or about 17th or 18th June, 1991, he was instructed by AE-2 to disconnect the electric line of Distillers Trading Corporation, Madipur, New Delhi at once. Mritunjay apprehended danger to his life in implementing these orders and he wanted to seek police protection but AE-2 did not help him knowing fully well that Mritunjay was a new appointee and had no experience of dealing with such matters. AE-2 brought to bear so much pressure upon him that he tried in vain once or twice to disconnect the line. In the meanwhile the consumer obtained a stay order. On seeing the stay, AE-2 became very furious and told Mritunjay that he did not disconnect the line on time and thus Mritunjay had deprived him (AE-2) of Rs. 10,000.00

"AE-2 threatened that earlier also he had got suspended another Electrical Inspector who could not arrange money for him and if he (Mritunjay) did not care, he will also meet the same fate." (The Statesman, Delhi, January 4, 1992).

This is how the corrupt DESU functions in the heart of India's capital—Delhi—at the ruination of the interests of consumers. But who cares? The honest official commits suicide while the corrupt ones prosper under the nose of the law of the land.

The Delhi Electric Supply Undertaking (DESU) must improve its services to the satisfaction of the consumers. This was the message given to DESU officials by the Lt. Governor, Mr. Markandey Singh on December 25, 1991 at a function which was organised to mark the inauguration of a 220 KV grid station, costing Rs. 10 crore.

DESU's transmission and distribution expenses should be reduced so as to avoid a high tariff. Only this will help to tide over the financial crisis. Power was misappropriated by the influential at the cost of the common taxpayers. The undertaking has to look honest in its own eyes and efficient in the eyes of the consumers. DESU could reduce its costs by decreasing the illegal use of power plugging leakages and bringing in corruption-free efficient functioning.

DESU should rectify faults in transmission and distribution of power. There is a lot which can be done to reduce the cost. This means the consumers will have to pay less. The increase in tariff has equally increased the number of people who now use power illegally through the corrupt involvement of DESU engineers. DESU's errant staff, whether holding junior or senior positions, should be brought to book for irresponsible and corrupt practices. Since DESU is a service-oriented undertaking, it has to be guided by the dictum that "the customer is always right."

Compared to DESU, the NTPC and NHPC are much more efficient in their working. The NTPC uses 1.2 ml of fuel oil per unit produced as against DESU's Indraprastha Station's 29 ml, it is told. Fuel oil is imported so it is a question of preserving foreign exchange. Power supply has been subsidised for the first 200 units of electricity consumed at home, to the Minister of State for power, the Lt. Governor of Delhi territory and other DESU officials. There should be no such subsidy and all must pay equally. By the turn of the century the installed capacity for the city will be 4000 KV. DESU's problem is with the software and the hardware. Software included manpower management, project implementation and proper enforcement of the system of collection of revenue. The real problem lies in improving the transmission and distribution.

The new grid hopes to benefit the four lakh population of Sarita Vihar and Jasola development scheme, various industries coming up in the vicinity, urban villages of Madanpur, Khadar, Ali Mithanpur and Badarpur and the adjoining rural areas. It also hopes to strengthen the supply to Okhla Industrial Estate, Kalkaji, Nehru Place, Govindpuri and adjoining colonies.

But Calcutta still continues to have the worst power record in the country. The Union Power Minister, Mr. Kalpnath Rai, has said that in order to increase generation capacity in the power sector, the government has formulated a scheme to encourage greater participation by private entrepreneurs. The country, according to the minister, had multiplied its generation capacity by as much as 48 times - from a meagre 1,362 MW in 1947 to 66,000 MW in May 1991.

The development of the electricity sector has been primarily the responsibility of the government. However, it is now clear that given the various constraints, the government would provide incremental capacity addition of only about 28,000 MW in the next five years against the earlier proposal of 38,369 MW. This would result in an energy shortage of 2.7 per cent and a peak shortage of 16.6 per cent by the end of the eighth five year plan. Under this background, the government has resolved to mobilise additional resource from the private sector. The scheme formulated for this purpose has widened the scope of private investment in the sector and modified the financial, administrative and legal environment to attract private entrepreneurs. An Investment Promotion Cell (IPC) in the power department has been set up which would directly interact with prospective private enterprise entrants.

However, on July 2, 1991, West Bengal State experienced its worst power crisis since the June 1990 grid collapsed. All the thermal and hydel power stations in West Bengal and Bihar collapsed after the transmission line between Malda and Farakka tripped around 6 a.m. And had it not been for a split second decision to isolate themselves from the Eastern region power grid, CESC would have been another casualty of the "Cascading effect" of the collapse.

The eastern power grid collapsed early in the morning (July 21, 1991) affecting normal life in West Bengal and Bihar. Only the Orissa State Electricity Board and the Calcutta Electricity Supply Corporation were spared since their systems had been isolated after a grid disturbance by way of an automatic mechanism. In a repetition of the crises last year on June 26, the Malda-Farakka transmission line of the NTPC tripped just before 6 a.m., setting in motion a domino effect. The plants at the Chukha hydel project were the first to be affected and soon enough those of the Damodar Valley Corporation and the West Bengal and Orissa State Electricity boards tripped. Within minutes the power output in the two states dropped to almost zero and desperate efforts to keep some of the generating units from getting knocked out failed.

The shortfall in the afternoon was around 800 MW. Frantic efforts were being made to revive some of the units, particularly the giant 210-MW unit at Colaghat and Bandel. Till late in the afternoon, the WBSEB generation was of 150 MW, including 20 MW from the Jaldhaka hydel unit and 18 MW from a gas turbine. The DVC's generation around 3 p.m. had risen to 200 MW and the CESC was generating 500 MW, although it was contributing less to the system. According to officials of the power department, an unit at Farakka, two 210 MW units at Kolaghat and one giant unit at Bandel had been revived. But there is an apprehension that several of the units may have been damaged because of the sudden collapse and repairs of these would take sometime.

In June 1990 it had taken over 72 hours to reactivate the thermal power units. But the cause of tripping then was over-drawal by Bihar and a fault in the NTPC-NAPC transmission line. The impact of the grid collapse was felt immediately in Calcutta with the All India Radio going off the air, trains on the Howrah and Sealdah routes getting stalled and tram services interrupted. Pumping of water and the major pumping stations were affected. Only the metro railway service remained normal. The situation in the districts is said to be much worse with the WBSEB generating only 150 MW of power and no alternative sources of supply available. After last year's (1990) collapse, a system of providing power to different parts of the state by rotation had been adopted in order to ensure that no area remained deprived. Earlier in June, 1991 (before June 20, 1991), a similar incident had led to the Kolaghat unit's generation dropping to zero. There was much concern that the two successive incidents inflicted severe damage.

Across the country, there is a contradictory quiet buzz about the Tata-controlled Bombay Electric Supply and Transport (BEST) and Bombay Suburban Electric Supply (BSES) companies. Their principals: Tata Electric Companies (TECO) have been facing problems that are almost worth the CESC's - not for three but well-nigh 75 years. Calcutta needs 800 MW of power. CESC has an installed capacity of 615 MW. This includes output from two antiquated units at Mulajore and new Cossipore. One is active since 1939 and the other from 1949 onwards. Ideally, the life span of a power plant must not exceed 30 to 35 years. Worse, the government arbitrarily fixes the installed capacities. So it can take anything between three to four years to obtain government sanctions for plants to modernise or expand them. "With all these restrictions, we produce about 500 MW", says CESC's Executive Director for engineering.

WBSEB make up the shortfall

The Goenkas have made good bucks, surely, CESC has grown from a Rs. 370 crore-Company in 1988 to Rs. 552 crore in 1991. Its share-holders get a 20 per cent dividend too. All very well in corporate terms. But the gloss is missing, the sort that makes TEC one of its kind. Thus, the private sector is not the answer. But efficient generation of power should be the goal. TEC started small in 1915, with a 40 MW plant at Khapoli. Now it has captive units in Bhirpuri, Bhisa and Trombay. BEST and BSES together produce 1,400 MW, while Bombay's remaining power requirement by 350 MW, is purchased from SEB. Managerially, they are tops, while the Transmission and Distributive (T&D) losses in the country run to 25 per cent. TEC has brought it down to between 8 to 10 per cent.

Experience has also made the company innovative. Their latest project confirms this. They are setting up a 150 MW Pump Storage Scheme at Bhira to provide more power at peak hours at more economic rates. TEC's success has not come easily, however, it functions under the Electricity Supply Act of 1948 that allows a privateer to function only as a licensee of the SEBs. Meanwhile, the reality of power cuts looms darkly over Calcutta, Delhi and other cities of India - and there is no controversy about that.

Meanwhile, a major power breakdown triggered by cascade tripping hit Bombay city and suburbs. Thane and Nasik districts in North Maharashtra were affected for several hours. The disturbance, according to the Times of India News Service on October 25, 1991, originated in the 400 KV line between Indore in Madhya Pradesh and Asoj in Gujarat accompanied by low voltage and low frequency which spread to the interlinking grid.

Power supply was severely disrupted for several hours in parts of Madhya Pradesh and throughout Gujarat following a major disturbance on an inter-state transmission line like the western grid on October 25, 1991. The Gujarat Electricity Board blamed heavy disturbances in the Maharashtra power system for the breakdown in all 25 Gujarat power units and parts of Maharashtra. In a statement issued late night from its head-quarters in Baroda, the board said the Gujarat units tripped because there was a dip in the frequency level of power supp-ly as a result of the Maharashtra systems disturbance.

Train service on the Central and Western railways came to a halt, production in factories and manufacturing plants was interrupted and work in business and commercial estab-lishments came to a standstill. Cascade tripping occurs in a grid when low voltage and frequency spill over into other networks causing a power supply failure in the interlinking system. The Tatas' Trombay Power Station in this instance failed to isolate Bombay from such a failure because the boiler of a 500 MW auxiliary generating unit No. 6 tripped leading to a total shutdown of power to the city and suburbs of Bombay.

The Trombay station, which supplies the bulk of Bombay's needs, is equipped with a mechanism described as "islanding" which isolates the Bombay network from such failures and maintains supply to the railways, Doordarshan, commercial and business establishments and domestic consumers. Their power voltage and frequency continued to drop domestically and generating units could not be run—even as auto generator systems tripped. Bombay received an average of 1,500 MW of electricity from Trombay station daily. The supply can some-time touch a maximum of 1,759 MW or a minimum of 1000 MW. Telephones went simultaneously dead and telephone calls could neither be received nor transferred outside in the sub-urbs. The power failure set off speculation that it was deliberately caused by miscreants probably at the behest of the Shiva Sena to prevent the public from viewing the finals of the one-day international cricket at Sharjah between India and Pakistan. Flights both at Sahar and Santa Cruz airports were not affected through x-raying of cargo at the Sahar air cargo terminal was slightly disrupted.

The power breakdown was not a major one, compared to earlier power failures. Last year on July 13, 1990, the state was plunged into darkness for a few hours as all the generating sets in the state electricity grid tripped and chaos prevailed in Bombay. The power crisis in 1990 was the worst in the state after that on November 20, 1989, when the subordinate engineers of the State Electricity Board went on a flush strike and switched off the power generating sets and transmission line. Another power failure on November 20, 1990 threw out of gear all activity in the city for nearly 3 hours during the morning peak period.

As a rule, the State Electricity Boards (SEBs) are a dismal lot. They are usually financially unsound with operational losses eating away at their performances figure. Till March, 1990 they were Rs. 3,265 crore in the red. But the Maharashtra State Electricity Board (MSEB) has a success story to tell in spite of frequent failure in power supply. How has all this been made possible? Productivity is the main thing, says MSEB Chairman S.P. Abraham. "Also the government does not interfere day to day. For our part, we make sure that there are no time or cost overruns." This has made Maharashtra an industrialist's dream state.

Indeed, even as the Centre was making up its mind about private participation, then Chief Minister Sharad Pawar had offered two major thermal projects to private entrepreneurs. There were a 820 MW gas-based thermal station at Raigad district and two coal-based generation sets of 210 MW each in Khopa Dkeda near Nagpur. Says Abraham: "The SEBs have no money. Then there is the power deficit. Private participation is long overdue. Since we have tasted the blood of industrialisation, we are all for it". And the results are there for all to see. Thus the role of the public sector would go down gradually with the increased participation of the private sector in the critical infrastructural sphere. It is hoped the response from the private sector, both Indian and foreign to the liberalised policies of the government should be encouraging. The Planning Commission's endeavour is for a smooth transition from centralised planning to a de-established one. While the role of the administrative machinery would continue, non-governmental organisations would be given assistance to grow. A task force has already been constituted in this connection. Priority would be accorded in the planning process to power, transport, communications and agriculture.

Drop in Industrial Output

According to the Economic Survey for 1990-91, the index for industrial production recorded a growth of 11.7 per cent in the first half of 1990-91 which declined sharply to 4.9 per cent in the third quarter and recovered to 6.0 per cent in the last quarter. The industrial production growth in the whole year hence declined only marginally to 8.4 per cent during the year, thanks to the first half of 1990-91, compared to 8.6 per cent in 1989- 90. The growth in a manufacturing sector which accounts for more than 75 per cent of the total weight in the Index for Industrial Production (IIP), also slowed down since September 1990. However, it increased to 9.2 per cent in the whole of 1990-91 from 8.6 per cent in 1989-90.

According to the Survey, the deceleration in growth of industrial production during the second half was due to several factors:

(i) constraints in oil supply,

(ii) infrastructure bottlenecks,

(iii) cut in government expenditure,

(iv) cost escalations,

(v) supply shortages of imported raw materials and components.

Excepting the infrastructure bottlenecks, all other reasons indicate that the Gulf crisis was mainly responsible for them to develop. Following the Gulf war, the country faced severe foreign exchange crisis because the oil imports from the Persian Gulf had to be made at high prices. This resulted in less imports but also imports of the raw materials and components were hampered. The Survey also pointed out that IIP registered a sharp growth in the first half because of a comparatively lower base in the corresponding period 1989-90. IIP which showed a decline since June 1990, recovered from November 1990 onwards. Since there was a sharp upward movement of index during the last quarter of 1989- 90, recording a growth of 16.1 per cent, the growth of industrial production during the last quarter 1990-91 was mainly modest 6.3 per cent.

Also the deceleration in the overall growth was continued only to the mining and electricity sectors. While the former's growth declined from 6.3 per cent in 1989-90 to 3.5 per cent, the electricity sector's growth came down to 8.6 per cent from 10.8 per cent.

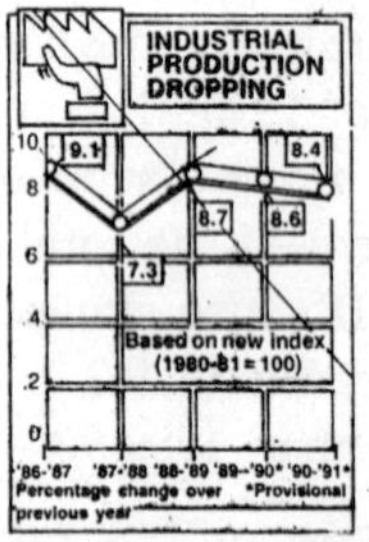

Out of the 17 industry-groups in the manufacturing sector, as many as 14 groups with a combined weight of 71.4 per cent with IIP recorded positive growth in 1990-91. Manufacture of electrical machinery and appliance (including electronics) recorded the highest growth of 22.6 per cent followed by cotton textiles (17.9 per cent), wood and wood product (12.6 per cent), food product (12.8 per cent), basic metals and alloys (9 per cent) and paper and paper products (8.9 per cent).

Production of three industry groups - textile product (including weaving apparel), rubber, plastic, petrolum and coal product and other miscellanous manufacturing industries - declined by 31.6 per cent, 0.3 per cent and 3.2 per cent respectively. An analysis of 155 selected industries with a total weight of 85.5 per cent in the IIP shows that of the 143 manufacturing industries with a combined weight of 63.1 per cent, 85 industries (total weight of 49.1 per cent), recorded positive growth. The industries which showed decline in the growth were pig iron, vanaspati, ferro-alloys, dicsel engines, millmade cloth, nylon and filament yarn, penicillin and tetracyclin.

The pattern of industrial growth needs a greater balance not only in terms of regional disparities, but also in terms of labour absorption and import intensity. Rapid industrialisation and its growth during the 1980s has not been associated with a commensurate growth in employment and has been characterised by an increase in import intensity.

In 1972, India's population stood at 563.9 millions. With the birth rate standing around 36.4 per thousand of population, the number of children born that year should have been about 1.5 millions. After adjusting for infant mortality at the rate of 132 and under-five mortality at 41.2 per thousand, the number of children surviving the school-going age should have been about 17 millions. With very marginal attrition in the ranks, these 17 millions would have reached the age of 18 in the year 1990. There will, naturally, be very great disparities between the educational attainment of these 17 millions. Perhaps 85 per cent of them would have been to primary school, though only about 30 per cent of the total would have gone through to the secondary stage. As for these completing their higher education, the number would be considerably lower than 5 per cent of the total.

Since 1960, the highest number of fresh jobs located in the public sector in any one year has been about 850,000. And this was in an exceptional year. If the average were to be taken since 1961, the number of additional work places created in the public sector has been about 410,000 annually. The annual contribution of the organised private sector to employment location has been about one-fifth of the figure. Within the organised sector - and this category includes all levels of government from the centre to local bodies - has been by far the more significant contributor. It may be assumed that of the total public sector employment of 18 millions, around 5 per cent falls due for replacement every year, on account of superannuation and other such processes. Then the job absorption on this account will amount to 900,000. The total employment potential of the public sector in any given year would then total about 1.3 million. If a 27 per cent

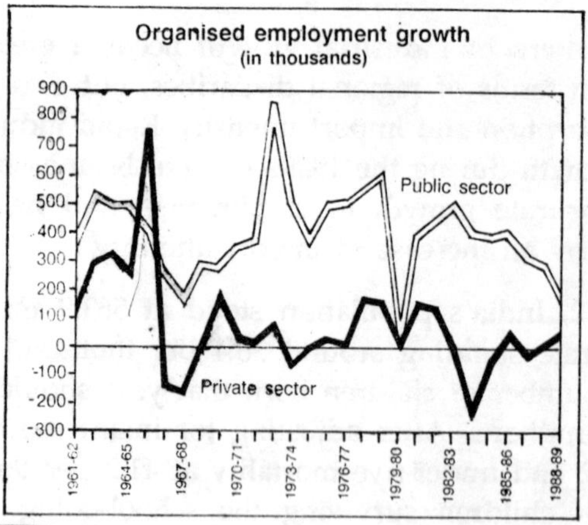

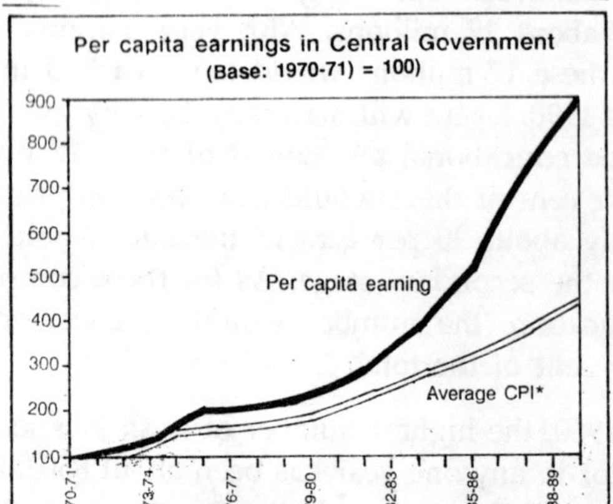

Source : Frontline, October 12-25, 1991.

reservations were to be applied to all jobs in the public sector—and not just central government jobs - then the number of work places affected would be about 350,000. If in addition, the 10 per cent reservation for economic backwardness were to be introduced, another 130,000 jobs will be affected.

Over the last 40 years, the industry and service sectors have expanded dramatically in terms of their share with national income, while failing to contribute much by way of employment generation. In the first quinquennium of the 1950s, that is, between 1950-51 and 1954-55, the primary sector, within which agriculture predominates, accounted for 56.4 per cent of the gross domestic product (GDP). Manufacturing industry and service accounted for the rest. In the final quinquennium of the 1980s, that is, between 1985-86 and 1989-90, the primary sector accounted for a mere 34.6 per cent of GDP. Industry and service have evidently increased their share in the national income, and indeed they should in a context of development. The rising share of industry and services in national income has not been accompanied by a rising share in employment. In fact, the combined share of these two sectors in total employment has remained virtually stagnant around 30 per cent for all of 40 years.

Meanwhile, per capita income levels in the industry and service sectors have increased rapidly over the last four decades, while agriculture has lagged behind, serving as a reservoir for the large numbers of people who are unable to gain access to employment in the other sectors. And within the growing sectors, it is again obvious that organised sectors would have done much better than others.

Government employment, in fact, has become an enclave of privilege in the midst of a generally depressed economic scenario. Between 1970-71 and 1989-90, average per capita earnings in central government employment have increased by the order of about 780 per cent. In comparison, the average all-India consumer price index has increased by only 340 per cent (as per the illustration). Central government employees, in other words, have been over-compensated for inflation almost twice over since 1970-71.

The mass-economic adjustment during 1991-92 may be expected to reduce the rate of inflation. But it could also lead to some deceleration in the rate of growth of production due to a reduction in demand. Such tendencies may be reinforced by the impact of the import compression on the manufacturing sector. In this context it is disturbing to note the deceleration, or even absolute decline, in the output of some key infrustructure sectors while, unless corrected, may constrain the growth of industrial production in 1991-92. Hence it is important to formulate precautionary measure to ensure that there is no significant deceleration in industrial growth. Nevertheless, it would be prudent to be prepared for a down-turn in the rate of growth of industrial production as a consequence of the combined effects of the foreign exchange crisis, the infrastractural constraints and the fiscal adjustment.

Infrastructure Sector

The performance of the infrastructure sector during 1990-91 was not encouraging. Electricity generation, production of crude oil and refinery throughout should evidence either of deceleration or actual decline. However, the railways maintained the same growth rate in terms of the revenue earning goods traffice despite loss of freight traffic due to civil disturbances, shortage of diesel and natural calamities. Production of coal and cargo handled at the major ports showed higher growth rates in 1990-91 compared with 1989-90. Within the power sector, the performance of both the thermal and nuclear sectors was poor while hydro-electricity generation exceeded the targets. The average plant load factor (PLF) in the thermal sector at 53.8 per cent during 1990-91 was lower compared with 56.5 per cent during 1989-90.

The production of crude oil declined by 31.1 per cent during 1990-91 mainly due to the agitation in Assam. Even refinery productions in terms of crude throughout declined by 0.3 per cent during 1989-90. The decline in the production of crude oil is a cause for serious concern in the context of the current balance of payments situation. Petroleum products play an important role in the supply of energy to different sectors of the economy. As per the latest information available non-commercial energy (fuel wood, agricultural and animal waste, wind and solar power) constitutes about 40 per cent of our energy supply; while commercial energy constitutes the rest. Within the commercial energy sector hydro- electric power constitutes only 3 per cent, nuclear power supplies only 1 per cent, coal and supplies 56 per cent and oil and natural gas 40 per cent.

India depends on imports of oil to a large extent to meet its domestic consumption of petroleum products, presently estimated at about 54 million tonnes. The cost of oil imports in 1990-91 which was projected at Rs. 6400 crore in April 1990 is now estimated around Rs. 10,800 crore due to the sharp increase in international prices of oil caused by the crisis in the West Asia conflict (Gulf War).

Some developments at home like agitations in Assam accentuated our difficulties in oil supplies. The short fall in domestic production of crude oil during 1990-91 is estimated at 2.4 million tonnes. Any bottleneck in the supply of oil could have a substantial effect on industrial output, costs of production and transportation facilities. Although there is some scope for inter-fuel substitution and conservation of petroleum, the possibilities in this regard are limited in the short-run. The area where the need for conservation and efficiency in use is the most urgent is the oil sector. There is an urgent need to check the growth in demand for petroleum products through a package of price and non-price measures.

Chapter II
Gulf War's Effects

India's refusal to condemn the Iraqi invasion of Kuwait could have lost India over US $ 7 billion in foreign exchange. This was the value of assets held by Indians who fled Kuwait after the last August 2 annexation. The only chances that India had of recovering this asset was when Kuwait had been liberated by the western allied powers. It was no secret that Kuwait and other countries hostile to Saddam Hussain in the Gulf had been displeased with India's diplomatic dillydallying. India failed to play any major role in the re- building of the region after the war. It was time India's foreign policy became more pragmatic. Before the Iraqi invasion Indians in Kuwait were sending to India over Rs. 900 crore in foreign exchange every year. This was apart from the Rs. 14,000 crore that came in from Indians working in other parts of the Gulf. After the crisis there was bound to be a lot of reconstruction work with the rest of the Arab World viewing the Palestinians with suspicion, it was unlikely that they would get jobs again. This opened up more job opportunities for Indian workers. Consequestly, this could solve our foreign exchange crisis—if the government could play its cards well.

Six months after the Gulf conflict, external remittances into the country continued to dip sharply, with the country losing close to Rs. 100 crore in foreign exchange every month. Also there had been a dramatic fall in the inflow of Indians living in the Gulf countries for summer vacation, as several workers in the region were unemployed for months experiencing lay-offs, and due to closure of factories and schools. This also resulted in a dry summer for most of the banks which used to cash in on a summer deluge of foreign currencies. Bankers also conceded that the foreign tourist's arrivals and their transactions in foreign exchange also dipped dramatically during the course of the year, and the country lost several hundred crores in the process. In the light of these indications, the new government at the Centre had a difficult task in mustering up sufficient foreign exchange reserves to see the country through at very difficult year ahead. Thus the foreign exchange starved the country. This seriously undermined the flow of invisible returns, which constituted between Rs. 8,000 and Rs 9,000 crore every year. These major setbacks to India's foreign exchange reserves occured even while it has been frantically knocking on the doors of the International Monetary Fund (IMF), the World Bank and other donor countries, to replenish its depleted reserves.

India had the largest contingent of immigrant workers in Kuwait and Iraq among all the countries of Asia. The government had informed the UN Security Council that it had two lakh Indian nationals in these countries, while Pakistan, Bangladesh and Sri Lanka had one lakh each and the Philippines 60,000. The serious crisis, which assumed alarming proportions with 1.72 lakh Indians who had to be air-lifted from Kuwait and Iraq in the wake of hostilities, continued to persist with hardly any of the returnees finding it possible to go back to their place of work with immediate effect. With the new government (the P.V. Narasimah government) assuming office in New Delhi, the Gulf returnees began to return to their original jobs abroad. While Gulf remittances to Kerala were expectd to fall by Rs. 300 crore this year, experts said that the short fall for the country as a whole could be as high as Rs. 1,000 crore. Kerala had close to five lakh people in the Gulf before the commencement of hostilities, who were remitting about Rs. 1,000 crore in foreign exchange. After the escalation of hostilities, 1.72 lakh people were airlifted from the Gulf, of which the govenrment of Kerala estimated, close to one lakh people were from Kerala. This resulted in a dramatic fall in foreign exchange remittances into the state from Rs. 1,000 crore to Rs. 700 crore. It is estimated that between 12 to 15 lakh Indians are employed in the Gulf, who remit anything between Rs. 3,000 crore to Rs. 5,000 crore every year.

The devaluation of the rupee had interesting sociological and economic implications for Kerala, thanks to its money order economy. In one stroke, the value of the remittance went up by about 20 per cent. This meant that the remittances from the Gulf which till the other day were worth Rs. 800 crore per annum would now be worth Rs. 960 crore. There were other NRI remittances for which figures were not available. The foreign exchange earnings through export of marine products and spice would be more in terms of the Indian currency. Last year 32,000 tonnes of paper were exported. Marine products were also exported in increasing quantities.

Several banks like the State Bank of Travancore, the State Bank of India, Bank of Baroda and the Indian Overseas Bank lost their zest for cornering more NRI and FCNR accounts. These banks had been the traditional channelising agents for the bulk of the foreign remittances into the country. Other sources of foreign exchange from the Gulf, like project exports and contracts for reconstruction were also yet to emerge in the full swing after the end of hostilities. The Overseas Construction Corporation of India (OCCI) and the Engineering Export Promotion Council (EEPC) began their visits to Kuwait. Meanwhile, most of the bigger project contracts had been gobbled up by firms in the United States and Western Europe.

Exports to these two blocks, which according to the Secretariat of the General Agreement on Tariffs and Trade (GATT) constituted 2.8 per cent of the country's exports, had also not limped back to normalcy. The Agricultural and Processed Food Product Export Development Authority was also stated to develop contacts with Kuwait as early as possible. Meanwhile, banking circles in Kerala conceded that a decline of close to 30 per cent continued to persist in inward remittance from the Gulf region. Officials of the State Bank of India in Karnataka said that the fall in remittances had picked up in the last couple of months, but still remained lower by 20 per cent.

India received the IMF loans of US $ 1.8 billion (Rs. 3,279 crore) to be able to pay for its oil and other imports. Besides, international oil prices were still low at US $ 21 a barrel and India was taking advantage of this contract for fresh orders.

Edible oil imports were continuing from South-East Asian countries. But the loan was not enough and India had to go to the IMF for about US $ 2 billion more. This helped India to survive, but added to India's crippling debt. Besides, only the US, or agencies where India had clout, seemed to want to give India money.

Despite imports, there was not enough petroleum products to go around, especially diesel and kerosene. Even aviation turbine fuel. The government announced fuel cuts for the civil aviation sector and the railways. Both Indian Airline and Air India cancelled some flights and reduced the frequency of many more. The railways pulled out 41 pairs of passenger trains, mostly on routes that used diesel locomotives. This affected transportation.

The storage of diesel also affected road transport. In states such as West Bengal, for example, trucks were sold only 50 litres of diesel a day. This affected the movement of goods. Even in Delhi, for over three months, diesel was not available. The capital of Delhi witnessed serpentine queues at diesel outlets. Trucks, lorries, tankers, buses, tempos all waited patiently for long hours, even days to have their tanks filled. And when their turn finally came they were told by the Petrol pump stations that supplies had been exhausted. So, these vehicles had no alternative but to wait for another day. Others moved to try their luck at petrol pumps elsewhere in the city. Most of the vehicles in those ever lengthening queues were trucks. And most of the truck drivers alleged that diesel was available freely in the black market. How does one explain if there had been a shortage of diesel, its free availability for Rs. 7, Rs. 8 and even Rs. 10 a litre (current rate of diesel in Delhi was Rs. 5.50 per litre) could get their tanks filled. These trucks transported house-hold effects, grocery, vegetables and fruits among other commercial items from Delhi to far off places in remote India. These truck drivers waited for diesel in Delhi and on their way to far off destinations, they would also wait at petrol pump stations for diesel. The tank can hold 300 litres, but the petrol pump owners rationed its supply upto 100 litres only. What is the attitude of truck owners towards the black marketing? Let things be as they were. Those waiting in queues also alleged that petrol was being sold in drums and jerry cans. The owners of petrol pumps maintained that such sales were permisable only for agricultural or industrial purposes.

Urban areas were the hardest hit—the rural areas were still more or less self-sufficient. Onions were selling for Rs. 10/- a kilo, double last year's rates. Retailers hiked price of most goods, saying the manufacturers and distributers raised theirs. There were numerous instances of black- marketeering in kerosene, and cooking gas queues were getting longer. Prices kept getting higher, but wages stayed exactly where they were.

Exports had been badly hit. Diamond, precious stones and Jewellery exporters reported cancellation of orders as well as a lack of demand in the lucrative markets of Japan. Europe and the US cancelled a leather and garment exporters. And engineering goods. There was also a problem with transporting these goods, as many airlines had cut or diverted flights out of India. Also, not many shippers were keen to pass through the Suez Canal, despite a major presence of US-led coalition force warships. The estimated foreign exchange loss was over Rs. 1,000 crore.

Tourism was devasted. Tour groups and conventions cancelled out and hotel rooms—even in Goa—were easy to find. The downshift in the trade started with the Mandal and Mandir/Masjid violence in 1990, in addition to problems in Kashmir, India's biggest tourist draw, but the Gulf capped all that. If it dragged on, tourist arrivals could drop by as much as half from the usual figure of ten lakh- plus. For the year 1990-91, the industry-tour operators, hotels, cottage industries - could be totalling up a Rs. 2,000 crore-loss.

Domestic investment slakened. Nobody, except perhaps the Nogajuna Group talked about setting up big project right then. Cut in oil supplies to industry affected production. The stock markets were in absolute funk and primary markets, which mopped up investment capital and served as tax breaks at that time of the year, were down and out. As far as share purchases were concerned, only the government financial institutions were buying. The automobile industry had been hit badly, even if temporarily. With the exception of the Maruti 1000, car manufacturers reported a further slacking of sale. Even the two-wheeler industry—which made fuel—efficient and less expensive machines—reported a piling up of stocks and slack sale. Only, the bicycle industry seemed to have any hope at that stage. The government was still broke, IMF loan or not. With reduced imports, reduced movement of goods and slack business, revenue collections—through customers dues, Octroi and sale taxes—did not pick up. The government also sent out circulars to cut its own expenditure, but nobody - unfortunately - was taking the move seriously. The budget deficit was still where it had been alarming: Both for the government and the public and it was getting harder still, especially for the public, as the government hiked excise and custom duties and slamped tax payers with a bigger burden. India had only Rs. 2,300 crore in June, 1991 in foreign exchange reserves.

The devaluation of the rupee pushed up the cost of edible oil imports. The net increase in the cost of import was around Rs. 25 crore. According to available information India imported only around 66,000 tonnes of edible oils in the first eight months of 1991-92. Though it was not known how much more oil would be bought from abroad, the total quantity would not exceed two lakh tonnes notwithstanding the actual estimated edible oil deficit of five lakh tonnes. The total import would therefore be appreciably lower than the last year's level of about six lakh tonnes over three lakh tonnes of deficit would be uncovered.

Edible oil experts pointed out that the landed cost of imported oil was likely to go up due to devaluation by around 20 per cent. Each one lakh tonne of the oils would now cost roughly about Rs. 90 crore at the current international prices. This would have cost only about Rs. 73.5 crore at the old exchange rates. The additional burden on every one lakh tonne import thus worked out to around Rs. 16.5 crore. Since the imports in the remaining months of the current oil year was not likely to exceed one to 1.5 lakh tonnes, the net additional burden would not be substantial, no more than Rs. 25 crore, in any case. However, some experts believed that the government could save on free foreign exchange by putting edible oil imports under the Replacement Licencing Scheme (REP). They ruled out the possibility of excessive imports as the landed cost of the imported edible oils, including duties and overhead costs, would be around Rs. 27,000 a tonne or more. This was quite close to the present domestic price range of around Rs. 29,000 a tonne, leaving little incentive for indiscriminate imports.

India could not escape the effects of the Gulf war over the next couple of years. Worse still for India—even if the conflict was resolved soon - was the fact that the Gulf zone would remain explosive as long as the region's oil lasted. Any upheaval there would always jolt India. Our country could be hit harder than others. India will have to remain careful in the future, as the Gulf, as a region, is extremely volatile and trouble could break out there any time.

Imports—not only oil—would be affected. There could be a shortage in edible oils, equipment for industry, and rough diamonds for the export industry. Shipments would be delayed. Exports would be affected in the same way as imports, most because nobody would be placing orders. Beside trade routes through Suez Canal would be blocked and aircrafts would have to by-pass the Gulf to take circuitous and expensive routes. Three-fourths of India's exports go to Europe and North America and most pass through the Suez Canal. Without much money from export, there will be practically nothing available for imports. Supply of oil to industry would decline. As it uses about 35 per cent of oil, this would hit industrial production. This will also affect agriculture and households, and as industry depends to a greater extent on these two sectors it will hit further. Exports may be reduced by Rs. 25,000 crore. Perhaps more. Either markets will begin to dry up or goods will not make it to the market easily. Income from foreign tourists will disappear. There will be no money to pay for import—oil, as well as crucial components for industry. Drugs even. High prices for petrol and diesel will hit transport. Supply of goods will be affected and even if trucks do move, their freights rates will be exhorbitent. Prices of every thing will rise alarmingly. Inflation could even hit 20 per cent. People will start hoarding commodities. Black marketing will flourish—especially in essential goods. The government will depend heavily on the railways to move goods, but as the railways can take only so much pressure, supply will remain short. Therefore, prices would go up. Panic will begin to build up both for the government and people of India. This could lead to some outbreak of violence. The trade deficit was Rs. 14,000 crore while the budget deficit was over Rs. 10,000 crore.

Power generation will be reduced, as a lot of it depends on oil. This will affect industry, agriculture and households. The combinations of less diesel and electricity to run pump-sets, less fertiliser and bad transportation will knock agriculture very hard. Good monsoons may not help much.

The Options

Mainly, because India imports enormous quantities of petroleum, 25 million tonnes of it a year out of a requirement of about 60 million tonnes. Most of it from the Gulf. Three-fourths of India's exports go to Europe and North America. The problem is the ships carrying them to have to pass through the Suez Canal, or if they are air-freighted, the planes pass over the Gulf. Imports crucial for industry follow the same route back home. Oil reserves were down to a month, said government source ("I cannot describe our exact oil stocks", said the former Commerce Minister Subramaniam Swamy, 'this is classified information'). Foreign exchange reserves were down to three weeks worth of imports. The economy was already spinning out of control and the treassury was close to broke. The effects of the Gulf war were disaster for India's economy and its people.

Because, things were bad enough already. Besides the oil and foreign exchange reserves, India's export growth rate dropped from 35 to 24 per cent, while imports increased—the trade deficit was already at Rs. 10,000 crore—plus. Revenue collections plummeted, while there was an alarming rise in expense for subsidies, government salaries and defence, among other things. Foreign borrowings piled up to such an extent that India owed the world Rs. 1,30,000 crore. Inflation hit 15 per cent a year.

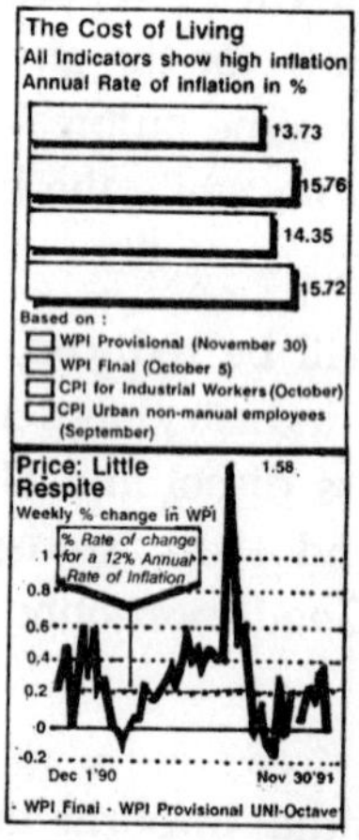

Source : The Times of India December 21, 1991.

Revenue collection short fall was Rs. 18,000 crore for 1990-91. Mostly was the result of government policy over the past decade. There was cause for alarm, anyway. The worrying filled down the levels. Any problem with oil affects transportation, industry and agricultures, however keen the government could be to salvage the situation. There was a direct impact on price, already rising steadily and expected to rise higher still. The concern about the future reflects the worry of every Indian, high and low. On the other hand, 1.3 million Indians in the Gulf, who sent home about Rs. 3,000 crore in foreign exchange earnings, stopped doing so - they were either out of jobs or had come back home scared. About Rs. 4,000 crore worth of project that India was executing in the Gulf—in Iraq, Jordan and else where—were put on hold. India could not get paid for them.

The international price of oil, which dropped to US $ 21 from US $ 28 a barrel in anticipation of a quick Iraqi defeat, could zoom up to anything between US $ 65 to US $ 100 a barrel. For this India would have to cough up an extra Rs. 4,000 crore. There would be no money to pay for this. Domestic production of petroleum could take care of a little more than half of the 60 million tonne a year demand—and the defence sector guzzled half the total anyway. Nobody could take the risk of reducing supply to the defence force in today's tricky environment. So, industry and the household sectors would be starved of oil. Industry would also be starved of investment and imports.

The hardest hit would be the petro-chemical industry, anybody who make synthetic fibres or fabric and the fertiliser units which use naptha, a petroleum derivative, as raw material.

As India has constructed more on thermal power to produce electricity—more than half the 58,000 MW generated comes from coal or oil fired plants - than nuclear and hydro-electric power, there will be a severe shortfall in power generation and supply. This has crippled industry to the extent of 60 per cent of its installed capacity. If there is not enough oil or if it becomes too expensive or supply cuts persist, transportation and the automobile industry—car, scooter, moped, even tractor manufacturers - will go to ground. Where the automobile industry was concerned, one hoped that the price of fuel would not shoot up. Because what was the use of a car, or any vehicle, when we could not have petrol ? Or trucks, when there would be no diesel ? Transportation would be dislocated and even if the government could manage to keep the railways running, it would not be possible to handle all goods and passenger traffic.

All these factors will have a detrimental effect on agriculture as well with no diesel, farmers could not use their pump-sets or tractors. With less power, they would not be able to switch to electricity. With the fertiliser industry hit, the productivity would also suffer. With transportation affected, crops could not make it to the market place. With people's purchasing power diminished, the farmers could not get good prices. And if the monsoons were adequate or if there were no rains, there would be no crops anyway. India's foodgrain stocks, currently out at about 20 million tonnes, would reduce rapidly.

There would be enormous shortages of food, fuel and money. Business would suffer, perhaps could go bankrupt, unemployment definitely would grow, but income would simply diminish. Hard pressed for relief people would go on the rampage. These alarming projections could seem straight out of a science fiction domsdayer's manual of destruction, but the fact was that the government considered these possibilities with the break of the Gulf War. This war was terrible. India was happy that the International Monetary Fund (IMF) loan was through for US $ 1.8 billion and not US $ 2.1 billion (Rs. 3,826 crore). That was a lot of money. With that kind of money at hand, the Government of India tried to speed up shipment of petrol already contracted for and arrange swaps. India picked up 1.2 million tonnes of petroleum from Venezuela, but that country was half-way around the world.

With the Suez Canal in danger of being shut down totally, ships had to take the circuitous route around Africa. So, India asked Venezuela to sell that oil to Malaysia (on paper), which had a lot of reserves. Then, Malaysia, much closer to home, could ship the oil to India, which it would try to pay Malaysia for. Malaysia, in turn, would pay Venezuela for the oil. No loss but oil gained.

Coal had been re-discovered by the Government of India. It planned to step up coal production in a bid to reduce the dependence on oil—for generating power, for use in homes (cooking gas was an oil field by-product) and, perhaps, even change the boilers in factories from using oil to coal. Or re-introduce coal fired steam engine in some railway sectors. There were also plans for stepping up the production of hydro-electric energy and the development of solar and wind power. And increase the production of domestic petroleum at Bombay High and Assam oil fields. The attempts for combat a crisis revolved around importing oil - of course, organising the money to pay for it—and substituting it. On both counts, there were major problems. For one thing, the money, even the IMF loan, would not last long. For another, the government may be successful in bringing down the use of petroleum products, but it plans with alternate sources of energy would either take too much time or too much money. Both in short supply.

Coal production was not increasing. It was almost static. Power stations had to generate more electrictity, but India was doing exactly the reverse. The plant load factor dropped from 56 per cent to 48 per cent. If this would go on, there was no hope for industrial development. A hydro-electric project would cost more money than a conventional thermal power plant - though in the long run, it was more cost effective—and India did not have the money to spare. More trouble. Bombay High and Assam oil fields were not producing as much oil as they should have—Bombay High suffered damage and in Assam, the effect of 1990's oil blockades and work stoppages had yet to be countered fully. On the other hand, a plant could not switch from oil fuel to coal overnight. It would take modifications in machinery.

Trade with the Gulf

The first casualty of the Gulf war was the price and supply of crude oil. Naturally for a country which imports almost 40 per cent of its crude oil requirements, and in the process spends over Rs. 8,000 crore of foreign exchange on these imports the price hike of petroleum products would be source of primary spiral in a Gulf crisis. In addition, there will be a cost-push in the myriad downstream by-product of crude oil ranging from plastic and dye stuffs of fertiliser and synthetic textiles. What happend a few months ago when crude oil price shot up from US $ 18 a barrel to briefly touch US $ 40 ? For the economy of India this time became more vulnerable. Indian economy was caught in a plight far from redemption. Oil industry experts believed that crude oil price could rule as high as US $ 60 a barrel in such an eventuality—and dollar increase represented an additional outflow of about Rs. 400 crore in foreign exchange from India. This would result in further adverse in the balance of payments situation.

The reduction in the remittances of the Indian workers in the Gulf area could be slashed by about Rs. 2000 crore on a yearly basis. The circle became complete when the domestic curtailment of India's exports worth of Rs. 1600 crore to the Gulf area became a reality. The final blow came when the fate of dozens of major Indian construction companies in the West Asia region with an outlay of Rs. 500 crore in various stages of development became uncertain.

India's Trade with the Gulf

Country	Exports (Rs. Crores)	Imports (Rs. Crores)
Bahrain	87.54	274.50
Kuwait	197.88	1160.28
Oman	89.14	5.60
Qatar	29.16	25.83
Saudi Arabia	428.49	1447.99
UAE	709.87	1448.42
Iraq	125.74	461.39
Total	1668.62	4823.90

Source : *Illustrated Weekly of India*, January 19-20, 1991.

At the same time, the single bright ray of hope became evident among India's construction companies that they would be able to involve themselves, in the re-construction of the war-torn and devasted Gulf economies. But in India, the Gulf was made its people bled through taxation and higher prices. Nevertheless, it really opened up fresh opportunities for those who dared to plunge themselves into the shattered Gulf region for its re-construction and rehabilitation of their people, Meanwhile, the Persian Gulf has been woefully polluted. Burning of oil wells are further degrading a fragile global eco-system. The Middle-Eastern arms trade has expanded. Yet, more of the above, including the waste of US $ 60 billion, are the major costs of the Gulf war. The ultimate price relates to the rehabilitation of war making as an appropriate method of resolving conflicts between nation states. the Persian Gulf war may be a portent for the 21st century in which savage conflicts over dwindling resources—be it oil, water, timber or whatever - will be resolved by technologically perfected slaughter of the 'loser' populations. These exterminations will be justified by misdeeds of the victims and will be propagandised and hyped as waging peace. Nearly 2000 years ago, the Roman historian Publius Tacitus saw through the rhetoric: "They make a wilderness and call it peace."

According to Bernard Lown, co-president of the International Physicians for the prevention of Nuclear War the Gulf war hijacked America's domestic agenda. Before the Gulf war there was a growing US national consensus for a large "peace-dividend". That demand is now silenced. The dawning of a new age - of swords into plow-shares, of burgeoning arsenals into shelters for the homeless, of lethal weapons into health care for the millions of uninsured, of arms factories into school houses, of military spending into investing in a decomposing economic infrastructure—was not to be.

The Gulf war restored the war-ped social priorities of the confrontation era. Gaining wide currency is the delusory belief that military power can solve the world's problems. Military budgets are once again robust. Exotic weapons are back in the drawing board. The militarisation of priorities is not limited to the US. NATO has also decided to get into the act. A corps-size formation of between 70,000 and 100,000 troops is being formed and on the ready as a rapid strike force for Third World emergencies. The affluent nations aim to maintain a global order of inequities, and NATO is gearing up as a participant. The US Congress is moving with dispatch to revitalise projects slated for dismantlement before the Persian Gulf war—for example, a new scale down version of Star Wars whose acronym is GPALS, which stands for Global Protection Against Limited Strike. This small programme is budgeted at US $ 40 billion and would violate the Anti-Ballitic Missile treaty, one of the major accomplishments of the arms control era.

Chapter III

Export-Import Performances

India's Exports had fallen in dollar terms in the first four months of the financial year 1991-92, partly because of the global recession, partly because of the major disruption in trade with the Soviet Union and partly because of the huge cash margins and physical curbs placed by the RBI on imports. Import compression was necessary to prevent the country's foreign exchange reserves from evaporating but it greatly affected inputs that went into exports too, showing how closely imports and exports were now related in the medium run India could service its debts only by expanding exports, not just compressing imports and so the RBI curbs must be lifted. The RBI felt it could do so only after the foreign exchange coffers were replenished by the next IMF loan of $ 2.2 billion, expected at the end of October, 1991. Till then it had pruned cash margins from 200 per cent to 150 per cent (which was still very high), and increased the list of exemptions.

More important, it raised the refinance available to banks to provide export credit. The new credit policy should be seen as an exercise in crisis management, which must give way to growth—oriented management in due course. As soon as inflation was controlled, interest rates will be brought down from their current stratospheric heights, credit for domestic production must be eased and the fullest freedom given for export production.

Ultimately, the debt crisis could be solved only by efficient growth, not by curbing imports and production. "We have taken the plunge and there is no going back now. I am prepared to go any distance and provide policy support on all matters which are necessary for exports to grow". This assurance was given by the Prime Minister Mr. P.V. Narasimha Rao, to exporters while inaugurating the silver-Jubilee celebrations of the Federation of Indian Export Organisations (FIEO) on October 7,1991. All biases against exports, especially in the government must be removed. The time has come to remove all import curbs. The cash margin requirements should be reduced. The interest rates presently applicable on credit should be given to exporters. These things have to come down and the quantum of export credit should go up. The policy measures are not only radical but also revolutionary even though the benefits of the policy measures would start showing only from 1992.

There was a silver lining in the declining exports in the first four months of the financial year 1991-92. There was a decline of 51 per cent in exports to rupee payments area but exports to GCA countries have gone up by 6 per cent. Over the last nine months of the financial year 1991-92 the government projection is that there would be a 16 per cent increase in exports to GCA. However, there is no scope for complacency. Referring to inflation, the government has said the advantage of the trade policy will be negated if the inflation rate crept up. In this context, everyone concerned should think and act rationally. Irrational behaviour will give only short-term benefits, putting the long term interests at stake. "Let us not put all our eggs in one basket. What is needed today for India may not be needed tomorrow." India should mop up every possible dollar from overseas.

Over the 1980s, fiscal deficits have risen sharply, resulting in an acceleration of imports and faster accumulation of both domestic and external debt. While the import substitution policies followed over the decade, have helped in locating a well- diversified industrial structures, the country's long term export performances has been dismal as shown by the steady loss of its share in world exports. Thanks to the protection provided by quantitative import restrictions and high custom tariffs, and inadequate competition even in the domestic domain, industry has not attained requisite levels of international competitiveness. It has concentrated on meeting, largely on its own terms regarding quality and price, the growing domestic demand to the relative neglect of exports which it found less attractive.

Over the last decades, exports and imports averaged about 5 per cent and 8.4 per cent of GDP respectively. These averages did not change significantly as between the Sixth and the Seventh Plan periods. The volume of exports rose by 6.8 per cent per annum in the first four years of the Seventh Plan as compared with 2.7 per cent over the Sixth plan. In fact, during the three years 1986-87 to 1988-89, the average export volume growth exceeded 9 per cent which was a record. However, the trade deficit remained higher or the volume of imports grew by 9.8 per cent per annum in the Seventh Plan as against 6.9 per cent in the previous plan period. Import growth in the Seventh plan was still higher if the growing disparity between Reserve Bank's BoP data and the Commerce Minister's import-export data are taken into account India's trade deficit during 1990-91 amounted to Rs. 10,644 crore, indicating an increase of 37.7 per cent over the previous year. This was mainly due to a slow down in export growth, according to the annual report of the Commerce Ministry. The report growth, will, however, return to the level prevalent between 1986 and 1990, if exporters take full advantage of the new policy framework. The viability of the Balance of Payments (BoP) position in the current (1991-92) and subsequent year will depend crucially on the country's ability to contain import and improve the export performance.

In contrast to the trends prevailing from 1986-87 to 1989-90 India's export growth during 1990-91 was particularly disappointing. The country's exports during the year amounted to Rs. 32,527 crore, as compared to Rs. 27,681 crore during 1989-90 a growth rate of 17.5 per cent. At the same time India's imports were higher by 21.9 per cent in 1990-91, as compared to 1989-90. The trade deficit during 1990-91 was Rs. 10,644 crore, which was 37.7 per cent higher when compared to 1989-90.

Exports by the State Trading Corporation (STC) fell sharply from Rs. 393 crore to Rs. 359 crore during 1990-91, as compared to Rs. 752 crore in 1989-90. The total turnover of the STC declined marginally to Rs. 1,819 crore in 1990-91 from Rs. 1,855 crore in the previous year. The STC's channelised exports also declined from Rs. 135 crore in 1989-90 to Rs. 114 crore in 1990-91. However increase over the previous year's exports were achieved for items like sugar, alcohol, molasses and opium. Non- channelised exports declined from Rs. 262 crore in 1989-90 to Rs. 167 crore because of the lower export of rice, coffee, spice, caster oil, leather, chemicals, sports goods and consumer products.

The Gulf crisis adversely affected the export of a number of items. Lower exports to the USSR, because of the restructuring of trading organisations in that country, were also responsible for the fall in exports through STC. A comprehensive plan has been worked out to increase the total turnover of the STC from Rs. 1,819 crore in 1990-91 to Rs. 1,950 crore in 1991-92. Exports have been targeted at Rs. 640 crore in 1991-92 as against Rs. 359 crore last year. A four-point strategy has been drawn up by the STC to achieve the desired objective during the current financial year 1991-92.

Imports in the country remained unbalanced, with nearly half the importers, accounting about 2 per cent share in gross imports, while then 5,000 importers, each having imported goods worth more than Rs. 25 lakh claimed almost 92 per cent of the value of gross imports. This is the conclusion of a study by the Institute for Studies in Industrial Development (ISID), which said a distribution of the country's import consigments, numbering 4.76 lakh with a gross value of Rs. 16,400 crore, showed a "high degree of skewness". Stating that the degree of concentration increases considerably when the consignments are tabulated in terms of importers, it said that on one exterme, need, half of the importers, numbering 14,615 had about 2 per cent share in gross import and on the other less then 5,000 importers, each having imported goods worth more than Rs. 25 lakh, claimed 92 per cent of the value of gross imports. The study said large private sector-importers, each with imports in excess of Rs. one crore, numbered only 1,481, but their share in the private was more than 72 per cent.

The study said large monopoly houses claimed lion's share in gross value of Indian imports and business groups and families, numbering nearly 200, accounted for nearly half of the gross imports to India. End-user classification of imports showed that synthetic textiles, consumer electronics, light automobiles and trading claimed a large part of the total. The Birlas, Tatas, Reliances, J.K. Singhanias, Bajajas, Thapars, Mahindras and Videocons topped the list of importers. Futther, the study said a good majority of the large houses are net losers of foreign exchange. The top net foreign exchange losers included Bajaj (Rs. 120.40 crore), Reliance (Rs. 65.23 crore), L&T (Rs. 48.23 crore), Modi (Rs. 29.17 crore) and Mahindra (Rs. 26.40 crore). Pointing out that exports of large industrial houses involve intra-group transactions and not necessarily an improvement in performances; the study said the emergence of Tata and Iron and Steel Company (TISCO) as a major exporter makes an "interesting study". Besides chrome ore, which accounted for Rs. 21 per cent of its total exports in 1989- 90, items purchased for resale by the company, amounting to Rs. 21.32 crore, included coffee, shrimps, pepper. The company exported rolls made by Tata Yodogawa, and pre- stressed concrete wires and tyre bead wires produced by Special Steels limited, its subsidiary. Exports of steel tubes are from the steel tube division famed after the amalgamation of Indian Tube Co. Ltd. While Tata Export claimed to export Tata vehicles, the daily trade registers (DTR) of customs house data analysed by the study asked whether it is possible that the vehicle exports are actually undertaken by TELCO and a part of it is "credited to Tata Exports to enable it to claim export trading house status and the concomitant benefits. If so, the study said, it is nothing but a book entry and in terms of exports there is no net addition as far as the country is concerned. The study said if even large houses had to rely on "general" items for exports in which they do not have any advantage over small and medium units, a review of the plethora of fillips for the trading houses stand should be made.

Despite the robust export performance during the Seventh plan period, a burden of medium-term factors such as the declining self-sufficiency in crude oil and petroleum products, the erosion of surprise in the invisible account an unfavourable climate for external assistance, and the bunching of debt service obligations, have continued to strain the external payments position, while the problem has been exacerbated by a number of short-term factors. The already fragile balance of payments situation came under intolerable strain in 1990-91 because of the Gulf crisis. This is reflected in the rapid erosion of foreign exchange reserves during 1990-91.

The Crux of the BoP Problem

India's balance of payments (BoP) situation remained under a considerable pressure throughout the Seventh Plan period, despite a buoyant trend in exports. Exports in rupee terms increased by 25.9 per cent in 1987-88, 29.1 per cent in 1988-89 and 36.8 per cent in 1989-90 On the other hand, imports recorded on increase of 10.7 per cent in 1987-88, 26.9 per cent in 1988-89 and 25.4 per cent in 1989-90. The Gulf crisis imposed an additonal burden during 1990-91 in the form of a higher POL import bill, a decline in exports, and also a possible decline in the inflows of remittances form the West-Asian region. In terms of rupees, exports registered a growth of 17.5 per cent in 1990-91, while imports recorded a relatively higher growth at 21.9 per cent. Consequently, the trade deficit increased by 38 per cent Rs. 7,735 crore during 1989-90. to Rs. 10,644 crore during 1990-91. Net invisibles are also estimated to have declined during the year due to a likely fall in the net private transfer on account of the Gulf crisis, a relatively slow growth of tourist traffic and a steady increase in interest payments on past borrowings. In the capital account, net aid disbursements in 1990-91 were higher than that during the previous years. Available information on other items of capital account also confirms the severe strain on the balance of payments.

The crux of the balance of payments problem during the recent years has been the large and persistent trade deficit and the declining capacity of invisible to finance this deficit. Net invisible as a percentage of GDP declined from an average of 2.2 per cent during the Sixth plan to 1 per cent during the Seventh Plan, while the trade deficit as a percentage of GDP declined only marginally from an average of 3.4 per cent to 3.2 per cent over the same period. Consequently, the current account deficit which needs to be financed through capital receipts, increased from an average of 1.3 per cent of GDP in the Sixth plan to 2.2 per cent of GDP during the Seventh Plan.

These growing deficits on the external account have had to be financed through large capital inflows, predominantly in the form of loan assistance from multinational and bilateral sources, external commercial borrowings including short term accommodation, and bank deposits of non-resident Indians (NRIs). Apart from the rapid increase in external debt that such financing has involved the average roots of interests thereon has risen while average maturity has shortened concessional flows have declined as the portion of loans at market-related rates has fallen sharply in the total provided by the World Bank. The net flow of commercial bilateral funds remain low. While annual commitment of external assistance has stayed at satisfactory levels, there are considerable lags in its utilisation due to delays in implementation of assisted projects. The share of external commercial borrowing and NRI bank deposits (which are both costly and sensitive changes in the environment) in the country's external liabilities has risen sharply in recent years.

According to Economic Survey 1990-91 external assistance during the Seventh plan provided 29 per cent of the financing needs, commercial borrowings 25 per cent, NRI bank deposits 23 per cent, and the capital transactions about 13 per cent. The balance 11 per cent of the requirement was met by the use of reserves.

The balance of payments situation will continue to be very difficult in 1991-92 despite the softening of oil prices in the world market. The respite offered by the IMF loan, under the CCFF and the first credit traunche of a stand by arrangement for three months was short lived. The crisis of credit worthiness and the erosion of international confidence during the past few months has accelerated the problem by limiting the access to medium term borrowing in international capital markets. Hence, even with a substantial import compression the pressures on the balance of payments are likely, to persist through the current financial year 1991-92.

In managing the balance of payments situation, it is essential to reduce the current account deficit in the medium term. It is not possible to achieve a sustainable solution to the problem without either. At a macro-level, in the medium term, it would be possible to reduce the current account deficit only by reducing the fiscal deficit. But a reduction in the fiscal deficit would lead to a reduction in the current account deficit with a time-lag. In the interim, it would be necessary to manage the balance of trade situation and to finance the current account-deficit.

The balance of trade would continue to be the most important determinant of the capacity of the economy to manage the problem both in the short term and with medium term. It is that a strong emphasis is placed on a rapid and sustained growth in the volume and value of exports. The policies necessary to assure such a performance must command the highest priority. At the same time, it is necessary to formulate trade policies in a manner that discourages import intensive industrialisation and foster efficient import substitution. Even though the planned fiscal correction should help in reducing import demand, it will remain necessary to continue with produce in the sphere of non-oil import. The same restraint would have to be exercised in respect of cannalised bulk imports. In this context, it is also of utmost importance that the growth in the domestic consumption of petrol products in 1991-92, as also beyond, is curbed as much as possible.

There is a danger that decline and stabilisation of world oil prices could locate a source of complacency. Given the near stagnation in the domestic production of crude oil in recent years, and the expected short fall in 1991-92, any rapid increase in the domestic consumption of petroleum products is simply not sustainable.

It is expected that the adjustment in the exchange rate and the reform in Import-Export policy, at the beginning of July 1991 would help to stabilise the balance of payments situation in the short term and improve the balance of trade situation in the medium term. The exchange rate adjustment (devaluation of the rupee by 20 per cent) should facilitate the realisation of outstanding export receipts, as also remittance, and at the same time, stem the destabilising market expectations which were generated by perceptions about the exchange value of the rupee. With a time lag, it would also improve the balance of trade by stimulating the growth in exports and curbing the increase in imports. The enlargement and liberalisation of the replenishment licensing system would provide a new impetus to exports and locate a mechanism for the needed import-compression. In conjucation with the fiscal adjustment during the financial year 1991-92, these measures would make an exceedingly difficult balance of payments situation manageable.

Import Bill on Oil

During 1990-91, India's import bill on oil at Rs. 10.820 crore was 72 per cent higher than that of Rs. 6.273 crore during 1989-90. There was loss in export to West-Asia, particularly Kuwait and Iraq. There was also a short-fall in the remittances from West Asia due to the Gulf crisis. Thus the balance of payments situation was under great strain throughout the year. Thus despite sizeable borrowings from the IMF in July-September, 1990 and January 1991, the level of foreign exchange reserves (excluding Gold and SDR) which was about Rs. 5,050 crore at the beginning of August 1990 dropped to Rs. 4,388 crore by the end of March, 1991, and further to Rs. 2,368 crore by the end of June, 1991. The direct impact during 1990-91 has been estimated at Rs. 5,200 crore or US $ 2,900 million. Consequently, there was a sharp decline in foreign exchange reserves which had to be stored up by recourse to IMF's compensatory and contingency financing facility and the first credit tranche of a stand-by arrangement aggregating US $ 1,786 million (Rs. 3,153 crore).

In any projection of the oil scenario, two basic facts should be borne in mind. First, against the consumption of 54 million tonnes of different oil products in 1989-90, the Eighth Plan document placed the demand for 1994-95 at 77 million tonnes, which would rise to 101 million tonnes by the end of the century and 127 million tonnes by 2001-05. Against these figures of aggregate demand, the import component in 1989-90 was 19 million tonnes and it would rise to 27 million tonnes in 1994-95. As the domestic petroleum is likely to stabilise at around 65 million tonnes. India's import requirements would exceed 60 million tonnes within a decade and a half. Second, the pressure of depicting oil reserves and mounting demand are bound to push up price of petrol and petroleum products to much higher levels in due course.

The Eighth Plan

Increased financial assistance from international organisations, more bilateral aid, rising foreign remittance and noticeable improvement in foreign investment besides new confidence in bilateral government-to-government cooperation have encouraged the planners to feel that the Rs. 7,92,000 crore Eighth Five Year Plan will not be over-ambitious. The resources crunch is likely to be overcome unless peace is affected by a war like the one in the Gulf according to Planning Commission sources.

It is pointed out that major oil discoveries like the Bombay High in the 1970s helped India solve its grave economic difficulties in that decade but the petroleum consumption has been rising very fast and crude production falling recently. India has very little cushion just now inspite of some good oil discoveries recently and plans to push up petroleum production by 20 million tonnes to 50 million tonnes in five years. But that will still leave India as short of oil as today and there is no sign of import being less than Rs. 15,000 crore or more every year for the rest of the decade.

It is for this reason that the planners and the petroleum ministry as well as oil and Natural Gas Commission have decided to do everything to find more and produce more petroleum through quick pacts with foreign and Indian private sector to avert the severe impact of possible oil shocks from West Asian sources. The Oil and Natural Gas Commission has decided to take the help of private firms including foreign one, to undertake intensive drilling operations in 72 blocks of oil and gas fields to step up domestic crude production. This was part of the government's and the ONGC's effort to increase crude production in the next five years. The terms and conditions of the fourth round bids for oil exploration have been finalised. The work of awarding contract to those firms will be finalised after opening of tenders and the oil drilling will start by April, 1992.

In areas where oil has already been found, ONGC will continue to work while foreign companies will be allowed to commence exploratory drilling in other areas at their own risk. ONGC has also signed a contract with Sri Lanka for drilling exploratory work. The Eighth Plan exploration strategy envisaged intensive exploration in categroy I basins like Bombay off-shore, Cambay and Upper Assam. High priority is also being accorded to exploration in the Krishana-Godavari, Cauvery and Part of Assam-Askam basins which have recently been up-graded to category I. The government has approval of Rs. 7,000 crore for the 2000 Flaring projects, envisaging effective utilisation of natural gas available in the Bombay High. The Asian Development Bank has agreed to give aid worth US $ 300 million for the second phase development of Gandhar South of Cambay Basin, which will cost Rs. 1,245 crore and has been approved by the public investment board.

The terms and conditions for bidding in the fourth-round oil exploration by foreign and Indian companies envisage a profitable sharing formula based on net cumulative cash flow of the total exploration and development costs. This formula is considered attractive enough to lure a large number of international oil giants of this country. The other aspects designed to attract foreign companies in efforts to speed up oil prospecting are said to be on a par with those offered by countries like China. The alternative in respect cf the share of profit will be post-tax rate of return. Foreign companies agreeing to transfer technology to the government or its nominess will be accorded preference. Besides, the government will permit remittance of such amounts as may be due to the company under the contract. The thinking in the P.V. Narasimha Rao Government is that it is time "we get out of a particular mindset", realising the urgent need to locate hydro-carbon reserves in various sedimentary basins in the off-shore and on-shore areas of the country.

Meanwhile oil imports on a small scale have been arranged from China and Vietnam and some other countries away from the Gulf. The feeling is that supplies from Soviet republics will stabilise again even though these will have to be paid in hard currency, but the effort will be to pay for them through massive project exports, especially in Asian republics. Zero gas flaring, it is stated, will not only step up power generation in the Eighth Plan but also give the petroleum sector more fund to use for exploration and recovery. The energy scenario is regarded as crucial to all-round growth of industry and agriculture and other areas of infrustructure, especially surface transport.

Even at the current level of import, a price increase of just one US dollar per barrel results in escalating the import bill by Rs. 400 crore. With imports jumping by 300 per cent in 15 years and the price of oil rising sharply, the out flow on account of oil import alone eat up all India's foreign exchange earnings and reserves several times over. This is a crisis situation which cannot be got over so long as our persent consumption pattern of energy continues.

Exploration and Conservation of Energy

The Petroleum Conservation Research Association plans to intensify petroleum conservation effort with an estimated saving of petroleum products' consumption equivalent to about Rs. 400 crore in 1991-92, through an intergated approach. A number of deliberate measures have been planned during 1991-92, for conservation of fuel oil, diesel oil, kerosene, LPG and lubricating oil.

The fuel conservation activities include 45 energy audits in selected industrial units with a consumption level of each of 1,000 kilo litres (KL) and more of oil per annum per unit, 250 fuel oil use studies and 1,275 follow-up studies with industries for implementation of previous recommendations, services to small-scale industries with annual consumption of up to 250 KL of oil per unit, through introduction of better housekeeping and management practices, assisting bulk furnance oil consumers- like railways, coalfields, steel plants, mining industry, etc. organising optimization studies of selected thermal power stations, using petroleum as a secondary fuel, and replacement of about 250 inefficient oil burners in various industries by fuel efficient low-excess air burners.

Diesel oil conservation activities during 1991-92 include demonstration projects like rectification of diesel lift irrigation pump sets, replacement of foot valves of diesel pump-sets, setting up model bus depots in State Road Transport Undertakings. Special stress will be laid on improving driving and maintenance control system. Thirty driver training programmes have been planned during this period.

In addition, in each region, southern, eastern, western and northern, training for trainers programme has been planned to be organised for State Road Transport Undertakings. BSF, CRPF, ITBP and Police departments, PCRA, in collaboraton with the Association of State Road Transport Undertakings and field teams, would assist in improving the efficiency of some State Road Transport Undertakings.

Thrust will also be given to the promotion of long drain lubricants and use of multigrade lubricants, modification in designing of automative engines, recycling of lube oil and assisting and educating users for creating the desired awarness. Promotion of fuel efficient kerosene wick stoves/LPG stoves for conservation of kerosene and LPG will be intensified. Mass awareness and education campaign through print, audio and visual media, seminars, symposia; workshops, exhibition, consumer meets and training programmes is proposed to be intensifed.

It is proposed to initiate petroleum conservation efforts in new areas during 1991-92, like shipping, in land water transport, fisheries through special conservation efforts in heavy and mining industries.

It is high time India should take note that after the first oil crunch in 1973, Europe was able to meet 95 per cent of its growth in demand by a more efficient use of energy. Even the United States, which is known for its profligate use of resources, strove to meet 72 per cent of its new energy supplies by conservation measures alone. As India, unlike the industrialised world, has reached nowhere near saturation levels in energy consumption, the need for us to tighten the belt all around is much greater. As nearly 50 per cent of the demand for oil arises from the public transport sector, maximum saving is possible in this area. Carriage of goods by road is the most energy-intensive and wasteful mode of transport. One horse power carries 4,000 kg by water, 500 kg by rail and only 150 kg by road. Yet, dieselised road transport has been increasing in India at a tremendous pace due to its efficient and quick delivery system.

Mr. K.G. Chaudhuri, who retired as a superintending geologist in the Oil and Natural Gas Commission (ONGC) in 1988 after having joined the organisation at its inception in 1956, discovered through his scientific studies the existence of crude oil reserves of 865 million tonnes in the oligocene sandstone stratigraphic traps of the Kathana-Kalamsar area of central Gujarat and 28.5 billion tonnes in the eocene carbonate reservior of West Bengal and the adjoining off- shore areas of Bay of Bengal. The oil expert's objectives then and now is given hereunder.

The central Gujarat reserve has the potential to make India self-sufficient in oil in a very short period and the Bengal reserve is capable of turning the country into a leading oil exporter and, therefore, the ONGC should not leave these reserves unexploited. The oil experts' battle opened an echo in Parliament too. In the Rajya Sabha on September 18, 1991, Mr. Sukomal Sen, CPI(M), making a special mention, asked the government why it was not taking steps to exploit these huge oil-bearing reserves in Gujarat and West Bengal. Of the 50 million tonne demand for oil in the country, about 20 million tonnes were imported involving a huge foreign exchange out-flow.

It is pointless to look askance at the government's decision to invite foreign companies to explore oil in 39 off-shore and 33 on-shore blocks in the country. Evidently, foreign firms did not rush in because they were offered difficult sites and not these with prospects of yielding rich strikes. The allegation by one expert that knowledge of vast exploitable reserves in Gujarat and West Bengal has been deliberately suppressed to serve vested interests abroad has yet to be investigated. However, there is no knowing when oil will be discovered and how worthwhile the new find will be. The best that can be hoped for is that domestic on-shore and off-shore as programmed from 32 million tonnes to 45 million tonnes in the coming five years or so. In this context, the current year's (1991-92) slide back in crude output is a cause for concern. Even if the country manages to catch up with the target, it will have to reckon with large imports to meet demand which is expected to rise from about 60 million tonnes in 1990-91 to about 78 million tonnes in 1994-95. The situation is getting worse day by day. Commercial energy, which accounted for about 40 per cent of the total energy needs of the country in the 1960s and 60 per cent in the 1980s, may account for about 80 per cent by 2005. India's demand for petroleum product may exceed 130 million tonnes by the same year. India's crude needs would be over 100 million tonnes just to maintain the projected levels of economic growth. India should take an aggressive approach for exploration in prospective basins abroad although India's local resources too offer the possibility of increasing crude output to well over the current production levels.

Petroleum Products Deficits (in million tonnes).

	94-95	99-2000
Light distillates	3.60	7.86
Middle distillates	14.47	26.33
Heavy ends	5.45	7.47

Petroleum Prices Hiked

The government has hiked the prices of petrol, high-speed diesel (HSD), Kerosene and liquefied petroleum gas (Cooking gas) in 11 states in accordance with the varying levies imposed by the respective state government. The increase has been effected through a hike in the surcharge to enable the oil companies recover the levies imposed by the state governments on petroleum products directly from the consumer. With this, the practice of the Oil Co-ordination Committee (OCC) reimbursing the state levies to the oil companies has been discontinued. The increase in prices has been the maximum in cooking gas, followed by petrol, HSD and Kerosene. Delhi and most of the northern states have been spared the increase in petroleum prices.

The government order was issued and communicated to the states concerned on December 31, 1991 but came into effect on January 1, 1992. The states where surcharge has been levied are: Tamil Nadu, Kerala, Gujarat, West Bengal, Maharastra, Karnataka, Andhra Pradesh, Assam, Goa, Orissa and Bihar. Condemning the unilateral imposition of surcharge on oil by the Centre, JACBOW threatened to withdraw buses from the road if the West Bengal government failed to effect an upward revision of the fare before January 7, 1992. The surcharge would severely affect the operators if the fare structure was not revised immediately. The price of LPG had gone up by Rs. 2.90 per cylinder and would now cost the customer Rs. 70.90. The cost of a litre of petrol had gone up to Rs. 17.17, an increase of 64 paise. In the case of diesel, the hike is 19 paise a litre, taking the price to Rs. 5.72. On an average, Tamil Nadu consumes 18,000 tonnes of petrol and 1.8 lakh tonnes of diesel per month. There are nearly 11 lakh LPG cylinders in use in the state. Petroleum prices went up on an average ranging from 22 paise to 24 paise in Bangalore, Mangalore, Belgaum and Mysore. In Bangalore, as per the new rates, petrol would cost Rs. 17.02 per litre, HSD Rs. 5.90 per litre and LPG Rs. 76 per cylinder.

The following table shows the extent of hike in prices (in paise).

	State	Motor Spirit	SKO	HSD	LPG
1.	Andhra Pradesh	12	02	04	47
2.	Assam	07	01	02	31
3.	Bihar	12	—	01	73
4.	Bombay Proper*	31	01	06	47
5.	Goa	09	—	01	—
6.	Gujarat	29	04	07	128
7.	Karnataka	22	01	06	70
8.	Kerala	110	11	34	512
9.	Maharashtra	31	01	06	47
10.	Orissa	22	03	08	97
11.	Tamil Nadu	64	06	18	268
12.	West Bengal	28	05	10	138

*The consumer in Bombay proper will have to pay this much additional to what has been increased in the whole of Maharashtra.

Source : The Times of India January 2, 1992.

The latest price hike in petrol from July 28, 1991 made it Costlier in India than in most other countries. This is doubly unfortunate as India has one of the world's lowest levels of per capita consumption of petroleum products and per capita income. The average price of petrol in the country's major cities is around Rs. 16 per litre, according to official sources. Comparative data on prices in the major consuming countries shows that in the United States, one litre of petrol costs the dollar equivalent of a about Rs. 6 only. Petrol sells at a litre over one dollar per gallon of Rs. 26 for 4.54 litre in the US. The price is comparatively high in Japan, where a litre of petrol costs the Yen equivalent of Rs. 10. In Germany, Britain, France, Switzerland, a litre of petrol costs less than Rs. 10. In Australia and New Zealand, petrol costs the consumer less than half the Indian price.

In many developing countries also, the price of petrol is far less than in India. The Indonesian price is less than Rs. 5, while in Bangladesh it is about Rs. 8 and in Pakistan about Rs. 9. In Argentina, the price is about Rs. 10 and in China about Rs. 5, according to oil industry sources.

Except for petrol, which accounts for only 6 per cent of the total consumption of petroleum products, the latest price of most other products are lower or comparable with those in oil importing countries as well as industrialised countries. The price of diesel in Bangladesh and Sri Lanka is Rs. 7.50 and Rs. 6 a litre respectively. It is in the range of Rs. 11 to Rs. 15 per litre in Britain, France and Germany. Diesel oil accounting to 40 per cent of the countries problem product consumption is priced at a little over Rs. 5 per litre in India. The country wide price differential in the latest price of kerosene (Rs. 2.50 per liter) and that of diesel oil and petrol may lead to widespread adulteration and diversion of kerosene, according to oil industry sources.

The extra revenue the government expects to raise to the oil pool account through the latest hike in petroleum products price is officially estimated at Rs. 1,600 crore in the remaining eighth months of the current financial year (1991-92) and Rs. 2,000 crore in a full year. The oil pool account had a deficit of about Rs. 1,700 crore in 1990-91, after transferring surpluses from the oil pool account to the general revenue to reduce the budgetary deficit in recent years. With the latest price increase, the oil pool account is expected to generate a nominal surplus by the end of the current financial year ending March 1992. It is estimated that the devaluation of the rupee costs India an additional burden of about Rs. 2,000 crore, although the imported crude oil prices are expected to remain around US $ 20 per barrel. The total oil import for 1991-92 are projected at 20 million tonnes for crude and about 10 million tonnes for petroleum product.

Co-Finance for $ 950 Million for Oil Import

India negotiated a co-finance facility totalling US $ 950 million from the World Bank, the Asian Development Bank (ADB) and Japan to pay for crude and petroleum product imports. The facility was being sought in addition to the US $ 500 million structural adjustment loan that the World Bank sanctioned on December 5,1991 and the $ 250 million assistance that the ADB to provide for the restructing of the hydrocarbon sector. The co-financing facility US $ 450 million from the World Bank and US $ 250 million each from the ADB and Japan - would be available over a period of 12 months in two equal trenches. It is being sought as a balance of payment (BoP) support to help India finance its additional imports.

As per estimate the country would be importing 20.6 million tonnes of crude and nine million tonnes of petro-products during the current financial Year 1991-92, with a total bill of about Rs. 13,000 crore. However, in view of the firming up of global prices and the high rate of interest applicable to India's oil purchase on credit, the import bill will go up substantially.

On top of this, India has to import additional crude and products during the current financial year (1991-92) because of the four million tonnes anticipated shortfall in domestic production. There has been about one million tonnes loss of crude production due to the disturbed conditions in Assam, besides slippages in certain projects in the southern region and Gujarat oil fields. Moreover, the Oil and Natural Gas Commission (ONGC) has commenced work on the closure of "over-exploited" Bombay High oil wells as part of its programme to rejuverate them.

The World Bank has stressed that India's crude and petroleum petro-product imports during the current year will be up by seven per cent. But the previous balance of payments position does not allow the financing of additional imports. The combined committees on Economic Affairs has put off a final decision on the prtroleum ministry's request for high imports till the required foreign exchange is tied up. According to an estimate, if the first tranche of the US $ 950 million co-financing facility is available, four million tonnes of oil can be imported. The second tranche then can ensure that additional oil import requirements next year are also met.

The BoP support facility by the Bank normally has a repayment period of 20 years with a five year grace period. It carries a variable interest rate linked to the cost of the Bank's borrowing. The co-finance facility would complement the objective of the gas flaring reduction project in Bombay High for which the World Bank sanctioned US $ 450 million in June, 1991. Also, the restructuring of the hydrocarbon sector, suggested by making funds available for maintaining oil imports. Sources say both the World Bank and the ADB have appreciated the steps taken by the government to involve the private sector in the development of the oil and gas sector and the cabinet decision to implement the Kelkar committee recommendations on gas pricing by linking domestic prices to the fuel oil prices in the international market.

Oil import calculations have also been upset by the division of about a million tonnes of imports from the Soviet Union to hard currency areas. Put together all these additional imports of oil will cost the country an extra Rs. 400 crore and that too in foreign exchange. Worse, the possibility that the need for additional foreign exchange in the current year may eventually exceed this figure cannot be ruled out. This is because the fate of the rupee payments arrangement with the Soviet Union or its various independent constituents remain uncertain. Even if the bilateral arrangements continue, the Soviet Union may, in the face of falling oil production, further reduce its supplies forcing India to import more from hard currency areas. The downtrend in oil production may also push up the price of crude abroad and make imports more expensive.

The assumption that the surge in oil imports in the current year is temporary and the import bill would decline once domestic production recovers is untenable. The fact that barring diesel, the consumption growth in other petroleum products in the current year (1991-92) is near zero as a result of the downtrend in industrial production and exports brought about by stringent import curbs. In other words, the demand for oil will pick up once the economy recovers. It follows that a relaxation of curbs on import would cause an increase not only of non-oil imports but also of oil imports. The finance ministry would do well to consider this linkage when it decides to do away with curbs on imports. The fact that the country has had to resort to loans to finance essential imports makes it clear that foreign exchange reserves, despite their recent increase remain way below their desirable level. For the future, the prospect of mounting oil imports poses a threat to current programmes of structural adjustment. If the government is determined to make a success of its economic reforms it will have to sustain investment in other sources of energy like power and accord the highest priority to conservation efforts to reduce the economic dependence on oil.

Natural Gas

The utilisation of natural gas to substitute oil's end-use, particularly in the transport and domestic sector, will reduce pressure on oil. India's gas reserves have been estimated to be around 1.4 trillion cubic metres as on January, 1990. India's current production is 17 billion c.u.m., of which about a third is unutilised. Add to the above the 13 million c.u.m. of associated gas worth of Rs. 700 crore, which is being flared and thus wasted. Hence, the scope for stepping up gas production is enormous. The government should formulate a plan to include natural gas use in the long term integrated energy plan.

Even though the budgetary share of investment for petroleum has grown from Rs. 162 crore in the Third plan to Rs. 12,628 crore in the Seventh Plan, allocations have been drastrically cut at the time of plan negotiations. It is estimated that 15.20 per cent of energy can be saved through conservation efforts and efficient use. If the efficiency levels had been maintained at the 1980-81 in sectors like freight movement by roads, increasing private transportation, etc. India could have saved over 4 million tonnes of crude worth over Rs. 670 crore in foreign exchange in 1988 alone. The savings will be higher now because of an increase in both the international crude price (by around 25 per cent and increase in rupee dollar parity nearby double). This can reduce the burden on the national transport infrustructures and reduce the cost of transporting energy.

The energy crisis has highlighted the dependence of the economy on oil imports. The need for energy conservation and the development of non-conventional energy source is clear. Although there is scope for energy conservation and inter- fuel substitution, the possibilities are limited in the short run. In such a context the utilisation of associated natural gas, which is flamed, needs immediate attention. This should be an integral part of management and the development of the energy sector in the medium term. The increasing oil import bill has already had a staggering impact on the whole. Thus the development of gas has become essential. The endeavour is to go in for a technology which would provide a substitute for liquid hydrocarbons. Out of more than 6 billion tonnes of prognosticated reserves, only 0.13 billion tonnes have so far been up-graded into geological reserves. Thus for the fourth round of bidding where a large number of blocks have been offered, the innerline clearance has been obtained from the home ministry on a case-by-case basis.

However, the crucial environmental clearance may prove an irritant to these companies bidding for prospecting work. The environment ministry has already declared that any exploration work should maintain a distance of at least 22.5 Kms from the boundaries of biosphere reserves or wild life sanctuaries.

Shortfall in Oil Production

Even as the government is trying to stave off foreign exchange "banktruptey" through an IMF loan, the unexpected rapid decline in domestic crude production could land the country in a worse balance of payments crisis in three years. If the oil production does not increase dramatically within a year or so, an implausible scenario to resort to yet another dose of massive borrowing to tide over the balance of payments crisis. Oil industry circles reckon that the Oil and Natural Gas Commission (ONGC) may end up with a short fall ranging from 33 million tonnes to 39 million tonnes during the Eighth Plan. At current price, this will cost Rs. 12,00-14,000 crore in foreign exchange. In November 1990, the ONGC management had proposed a downward revision of its Eighth Plan target by 6.32 million tonnes. The government has not yet agreed to this.

When questioned as to whether the company could achieve the reduced cumulative production target of 183.32 million tonnes (compared to 145.72 million tonnes in the Seventh Plan), the ONGC management evaded the issue by stating, "Everything is in a flax as the government has not yet taken a decision on its revised prduction target."

ONGC had originally fixed and officially communicated to the government a production target of 189.64 million tonnes for the on-going plan period. This means an increase of 44 million tonnes over that of the Seventh Plan cumulative production.

Company insiders maintain that not more than six to 11 million tonnes crude output over the seventh plan production is possible. This too is subject to the Neelam field in Bombay off-shore going into production by the terminal year of the plan and attaining a peak production rate of six million tonnes per annum in the fiscal year itself (1991-92). ONGC has already lost nearly three million tonnes in the first of the Eighth Plan (four million tonnes loss compared to the target fixed in the plan working group and three million tonnes compared to the target fixed in the MOU with the government. It is stated to lose another six million tonnes in the current year (1991-92). There is no indication that the trend could be reversed.

Sources in ONGC acknowledge that raising production from the present level of 28 million tonnes per annum to 46 million tonnes by the terminal year of the Eighth Plan is "simply impossible". At best, ONGC could end up with a production rate of 35 million tonnes in 1994-95. The present rate of production is four million tonnes less than the Seventh Plan terminal year production. It appears that neither the bureaucracy nor the political leadership has any clear idea about the magnitude of the crisis.

Almost all middle level officials in the field of crude production pointed a grim scenario. ONGC does not have experienced production experts at the top executive levels. As a result, production has been in the down trend. Inquiries reveal that the style of functioning of the top management has totally demoralised the employees. According to oil experts, the top management has lost its grip on production. Of the total of 530 wells in off-shore, as many as 154 are remaining idle, of which 105 are in Bombay High.

ONGC has so far produced only 45 per cent of the recoverable reserves per annum in Bombay off-shore and with the balance recoverable, ONGC should have been able to produce 32 million tonnes per annum. The present rate of production from Bombay off - shore is only 18 million tonnes per annum. Oil experts say that the government will have to take some hard decision with regard to ONGC to avert a management crisis.

Shortfall in Coal Production

There has been a substantial short fall in the production of coal. As against the target (even a singular collieries in Singareni areas) of 21.5 million tonnes, only 17.8 million tonnes of coal was produced, with a short fall of nearly 17 per cent. This was mainly due to factors like strikes, absenteeism, etc. It will be prudent to go in for alternative fuels. Since conservation efforts by the road transport organisations and industry will be minimal and can not be relied upon to make any serious containment in demand unless adequate fiscal incentives are given by the government. India has one of the largest reserves of coal in the world, which are expected to last for nearly 2000 years. Reserves of all types of coal were about 186 billion tonnes as of January 1, 1990. But of these, only 56 billion tonnes or 50 per cent were proven reserves.

Bihar seems well endowed with reserves of more than 61 billion tonnes, followed by Orissa (44 billion), Madhya Pradesh (35 billion) and West Bengal (30 billion). But though Bihar has the largest reserves of coal, Orissa leads in new finds. Because in 1986 and 1990, the reserves in Orissa increased by nearly 15 billion tonnes, which incidentally works out to 43 per cent of the total increase in coal reserves during that period. During the same period, the increase in Bihar was 3.3 billion tonnes. However, the bulk of the coal reserves is of the non-coking type, which is not very suitable for industries like steel and cement. It is estimated that reserves of coking coal are only around 50 billion tonnes. The Jharia coal fields being India's only source of prime coking coal.

Coal production, after its nationalisation in 1971, has been rising at a steady pace of around five per cent per annum. The total coal production increased by around 6.7 per cent during the Sixth Plan and by nearly seven per cent in the Seventh Plan. Production of coal during 1989-90 stood at 200.54 million tonnes and was up by 5.2 per cent over 1988-89. But this was short of the target of 209.5 million tonnes fixed for that year.

Coal India Limited Produced 178.6 million tonnes which incidentally, accounted for 89 per cent of the total production.

In the next few years, it would be prudent to put emphasis on the development of coal, as opposed to oil and natural gas, because of its easy availability. In addition, the government should make sincere efforts in order to adopt strategies to increase efficiency in energy utilisation develop technologies to tap renewal energy sources and place greater emphasis on afforestation programmes in order to attain substainable development without environmental degradation. By the end of 1990-91, there were 24 projects each costing over Rs. 100 crore under implementation.

Out of these 20 were in the coal sector and 4 in the high lignite sector. There has been delay in case of a project due to problems relating to acquisition of land, rehabilitation of land oustees as well as supply of equipment by local manufacturers.

Quality of Coal

In the midst of raging controversy over the import of coking coal, Coal India Limited (CIL) has accused the Steel Authority of India Limited (SAIL) of wasting foreign exchange at a time when the country's economy is under severe strain. SAIL in turn has held CIL responsible for supplying it with sub- standard coking coal - one of the chief raw materials for the production of steel. Towards the end of 1990, SAIL floated a global tender for the purchase of low ash content coking coal. The country then was going through an acute foreign exchange crunch, but SAIL managed to convince the government to import this premium brand of coal, stocks of which were extremely low according to the company. The Australian firm, South Blackwater Mines, bagged the contract for the supply of 75,00 tonnes of the premium grade of coal at the rate of US $ 59.91 per tonne. What's important is that South Blackwater Mines had earlier got an order from SAIL to supply coking coal, but this was cancelled because the product supplied by the Australian company had failed to meet the required specifications. Inspite of such a bad reputation, SAIL handed over a fresh contract to Blackwater Mines. Steel Authority of India sources said that it had to go in for coking coal imports because the product supplied by Coal India Limited was unfit for making high grade steel. CIL's coking coal had a high ash content - around 24 per cent which was well above the stipulated norm of 17.20 per cent.

In fact, SAIL's coal import bill over the year has been a cause for concern. In 1976-77, the public sector steel giant produced 8.1 million tonnes of steel without using any imported coal. SAIL started importing coking coal in 1978, and within the next ten years, it was importing around 30-40 per cent of its total raw material requirements. And in 1990, the company imported 4.5 million tonnes of prime coking coal and produced just 8.5 million tonnes of the metal. Which means that the country was spending around Rs. 550 crores in foreign exchange annually to keep the blast furnaces of its steel plants alive.

At present, the domestic reserves of coking coal are an estimated at 28,000 million tonnes. And going by the steel sector's demand of 15 million tonnes of the mineral annually, there is no crisis whatsoever. In fact, there is no dearth of high quality coal in India if mined properly. Raw coal mined by CIL normally has an ash content of 23 to 24 per cent, which experts felt could be easily washed down to 20 per cent. Moreover, the private sector Tata Iron and Steel Company (TISCO) has enough reserves of high grade coking coal in its captive mines near Jameshedpur. TISCO's imports vary between 10 and 20 per cent against SAIL's demand of 40 to 50 per cent foreign coal, steel plants can efficiently use Indian coal blended with the imported ones. But SAIL is adament. While the two giant public sectors squable in the open, the government can do little but sit back and watch. This is an investigative report published in **Sunday** 28 July- 3 August, 1991.

Coal Mines may go to Pvt. Sector

Some of the coal mines in non-congress ruled states are likely to be "privatised" in as much as they will be provided as "captive mines" to the power plants sanctioned in the private sector. The demand that these mines be attached to power plants in the private sector has been made by the Chief Minister of Bihar, West Bengal, Orissa and Rajasthan, according to Mr. P.A. Sangma, minister of State with independent charge for coal. However, the minister has ruled out the wholesale privatisation of coal mines which, he said, would continue to be in the nationalised sector. According to present assessment, five or six coal mines will be "privatised" to serve the needs of the proposed power plants in the private sector.

Later, at a meeting with mediamen in *Sharam Shakti Bhawan* Mr. Sangma, who is holding charge of the labour ministry as well, said that two status papers would be produced in a short period of time on two topics. One would be on how to survive the public sector units that are not doing well. The other would be on coal mines that are not performing well. Both the status papers were discussed in the tripartite meeting held in December 1991. The first such meeting was fruitful, cordial and the members present were responsive and positive.

In the heavy industry sector, there was a total investment of Rs. 99,315 crore in 244 units till March 31, 1990. Of these 244 units, 131 made profits of Rs. 5741 crore. However, 50 were showing chronic losses. Remedial measures would be discussed after the status paper on the subject was considered by the tripartite meeting. Of the 398 coal mines, 97 had made a profit of Rs. 991.50 crore, employing 25 per cent of the work-force and producing 3.74 lakh tonnes per day. However, 63 per cent of the work force in 251 coal mines produced only 28 per cent of coal with a loss of Rs. 1,117 crore.

Low productivity, poor management, lack of upgradation of technology and research and development were some of the factors contributing to the heavy losses in the coal sector, according to Mr. Sangma. Once the status paper was discussed, specific problems and specific solutions would be forthcoming, the minister assumed.

Coal India's Plan outlay Pruned by 30 per cent

Faced with a severe resource crunch, the public sector Coal India Ltd had decided to slash its plan outlay by nearly 30 per cent in the current year, with the Rs. 2035 crore capital expenditure target for 1991-92 pruned to around Rs. 1450 crore. Stating that this would be even lower than the expenditure of Rs. 1638.18 crore incurred by CIL in 1990-91, CIL sources said that the production plan of 203 million tonnes for the year, would not be hit. Areas where the investment cut were proposed to be effected were equipment procurement and new project. While existing projects would not be affected, new ones in almost all coal companies would be slowed down, especially where these were not tied to any foreign credit.

Among projects, where investment would be slowed down were the Jhanjra underground and the Kottadih projects of the Eastern Coalfields Ltd, and Pootkee Balihari and the Bhalgora of the Bharat Coking Coalfields Ltd area. In the northern coalfields, the Khadia project would have an investment of only Rs. 51 crore this year against the Rs. 83 crore planned. Other would be the Umrer project under the western coalfields and Belpahar of the south eastern coalfields. The sources said that the decision of these projects was taken after a close review. It was felt that there was considerable scope for rephasing of investment after examining their specific needs. The sources said that procurement of major equipment was expected to be far less this year, as better utilisation of existing ones and rescheduling of the purchase of new ones was being emphasised.

The holding company for the seven coal producing subsidiries was exercising strict control over costs and plan to save around Rs. 72 crore this year. Referring to the need for pruning the year's outlay, the sources said that although hopes for a price increase had not been given up, it would be possible to raise only around Rs. 350 crore through additional resource mobilisation, even if the price increase took place this time. Earlier it was hoped that Rs. 600 crore in additional revenue would come from the price increase, which had been pending for long.

Another shortfall in resource occurred when the government unexpectedly stopped budgetary support from August this year, after giving Rs. 399 crore, with Rs. 549 crore expected.

The resource gap increased further when there was a shortfall in the availability of bilateral credit from Rs. 213 crore to Rs. 133 crore, as sectoral credit from the World Bank, failed to materialise.

A Case Study

The World Bank gave ultimatum to the Government of West Bengal on funding on a coal mine project (Rs. 350 crore) in the Sonepur - Buzari area. The Bank's ultimatum came in the wake of a visit to the mine site by its team. The team found new constructions and cultivation in progress in 447 hectares of land acquired and fenced off a year ago by Eastern Coalfields Ltd (ECL). The land was acquired after paying compensation. But the former land owner knocked down the fence and took possession of the land. The team recommended to the World Bank to withdraw funds to the project as it would take years to re-acquire the land. In the event of this decision being taken, West Bengal's loss could become Bihar's gain. These funds of Rs. 350 crore would go to project in Bihar.

According to the World Bank team which visited the mine site on September 30, 1991, unless Sonepur and Buzari villages were immediately handed over to the ECL, the project was unlikely to take off and be completed by September 1996. This was after allowing for two years extention beyond the original closing date of September 1994. The ECL faced the task of retaking the land which it had acquired after years of 11 "politically sensitive negotiations". The team was also informed that the ECL would have to pay compensation to the farmers once again to take possession of the land.

The minutes of negotiations required that the remainder of the land should be acquired by the end of 1992. Also remaining to be acquired was the strip of land to accommodate the 11.7 km rail link to the Eastern Railways main lines. The World Bank team noted: "After four years of negotiations the route for this link has still not been finalised and land acquisition cannot even commence."

In terms of coal production, the setback could be substantial. The team's assessment was that it would not be possible to have the mine's target tonnage of three million tonnes, per year until the link had been established. Till then, only 9 maximum of 1.5 million tonnes per year could be evacuated via Gaighats. What had disturbed the World Bank team even more was the fact that the villagers of Buzari and Sonepur were still occupying their houses within the mine area. An area was earmarked for their resettlement but no steps had been taken. Though the villagers need not be disturbed for one or two years, it could happen that the longer they stayed, the more difficult it would be to move them out.

The ECL reported to the team that 320 families were still occupying 105 buildings and 220 hutments in Sonepur and 270 families occupying 210 buildings and 230 hutments in Buzari. Expressing doubts about the project being implemented on time even if the closing date of the loan was extended by several years, the World Bank team felt that the remaining funds be allocated to other projects. In case the World Bank will withdraw from this project, it would be difficult for the Centre to arrange fund for the Sonepur - Buzari project in West Bengal.

Lignite

Lignite production had been on an average by 24.3 per cent annually during the Sixth plan. The growth rate during the Seventh plan was however, only 10.6 per cent per annum. Production of lignite in Neyveli Lignite Corporation (NLC) which produces most of the lignite in the country went upto 11.76 million tonnes in 1990-91 against 11.23 million tonnes in

1989- 90. Some small quantities of lignites are also produced in mines managed by the Gujarat Mineral Development Corporation (GMDC). NLC has also recorded significant achievements within the field of power generation and is functioning as a model agency for the exploration of lignite deposits in Rajasthan, Gujarat and Jammu and Kashmir.

Electricity

Energy generation (total utilities in terms of hydel, thermal and nuclear) recorded an annual growth rates of 8.5 per cent during the Sixth plan. Of the total power generated, hydel power registered an annual growth rate of 3.5 per cent, thermal 12 per cent and nuclear 12.4 per cent. During the Seventh Plan, the total power generation drew at a rate of 9.4 per cent. Hydel power recorded a growth rate of 3.5 per cent, thermal power grew at a somewhat higher rate of 12.6 per cent, while nuclear power grew at a rate of 3.5 per cent per annum. The pattern of electricity consumption has also undergone change during the two plan periods. On the eve of the Sixth Plan (1979-80) 58.9 per cent of total electricity consumption was accounted for by the industrial sector while the share of agriculture was 17.2 per cent. However, during the terminal year of the Seventh Plan (1989-90) the share of agriculture has gone up to 2.5 per cent while that of industry has declined to 46.3 per cent.

The share of thermal power in the hydel-thermal mix has been steadily rising. At present, thermal power contributes about 69.8 per cent to the total power generated. There has been continuous improvement in the performance of thermal power stations in recent years. At the begininng of the Sixth Plan, the PLF (plant load factor) of the thermal plants was 44.3 per cent. It improved to 50.1 per cent by 1984-85 and to 56.5 per cent in 1987-88. However, during 1988-89., the PLF of thermal plants declined to 55 per cent because of lower agricultural demand on account of favourable mansoon. In 1989-90, the PLF had improved once again to 56.5 per cent, it went down to 53.8 per cent in 1990-91. The central sector PLF in 1989-90 was 62.2 per cent as against 62.6 per cent in 1988-89. The PLF of the state sector was 53 per cent compared to 51.6 per cent during the previous year.

The private sector PLF during 1989-90 was 69.5 per cent compared with 63.2 per cent in 1988-89.

The fall in the PLF during 1990-91 could be attributed to inadequate supplies of coal and backing down due to favourable mansoon conditions. The state Electricity Boards of Andhra Pradesh, Karnataka, Tamil Nadu, Punjab, Gujarat, Maharashtra, Madhya Pradesh, the West Bengal Power Development Corporation, the Delhi Electricity Supply Undertaking (DESU) and Uttar Pradesh Electricity Supply Board continued to maintain a PLF at more than 50 per cent during 1990-91. Private utilities achieved a PLF of 58.4 per cent during 1990-91 against the target of 58.6 per cent.

Thermal generation in 1989-90 was 178-7 billion KWH. This was 13.3 per cent higher than in 1988-89 but fell short of the target by 2.1 per cent. The short fall was mainly due to reduced load demand, particularly from the agricultural sector on account of favourable monsoon conditions. Hydel power generation at 62.1 billion KWH in 1989-90 marked an improvement of 7.3 per cent over 1988-89 and was equal to the target fixed. The nuclear power generation in 1989-90 at 4.6 billion KWH was, however, less by 20.7 per cent than the level reached in 1988-89 on account of problems in the nuclear power reactors.

The total power generation in 1990-91 was 264.2 billion KWH recording an increase of 7.7 per cent over 1989-90 at 245.5 billion KWH. Hydel power generation was higher by 15.1 per cent at 715 billion KWH. while thermal (including nuclear) power generation went upto 192.7 KWH showing an increase of 5.1 per cent over 1989-90. The target for additional power generation capacity in 1990-91 was revised to 4212 MW compromising 3970.5 MW thermal and 1006.5 MW hydro-power generation. Actual capacity rolled/commissioned during 1990-91 was 3776.5 MW, out of which 2331 MW was from thermal and 445.5 MW form hydel power. A capacity addition, of 22,245 MW was targeted for the Seventh Plan. Actual achievement has, however, been lower at 21,401.6 MW.

Chamera Hydro-Electric Power Project

The 540 MW Chamera project in Himachal pradesh is an example if the steady flow of fund to the project is not maintained, may be delayed. This Hydro-electric power project is being executed under the aegis of the National Hydro-Electric Power Corporation (NHPC), is targeted for comissioning in December 1992, but the schedule is likely to go haywire if the flow of fund during the current crucial stage is disrupted. Owing to the overall financial crunch, funds for the project have not been forthcoming from the government.

Even during low-intensity work schedules, construction of a large project like a dam is an waresome sight. The magnitude of the Chamera project is heightened as for the first time in the country some of the latest heavy machinery in the construction industry has been used. Most of this equipment has been imported from Canada under a bilateral agreement. Consider this: The conrete used in constructing the 765 metre high, 288- metre wide dam on River Ravi is enough to lay a two-lane road from Kashmir to Kanyakumari. So far nearly 3 lakh tonnes of concrete has been consumed. And, each of the 96 buckets on a 4.5 Km Cableway carrier concrete enough to build a two-bed roomed apartment.

If funds are not made available, this may also affect 120 MW Tanakpur project in UP. Some public sector undertakings are likely to surrender part of their funds in March, 1992 which could be transferred to the NHPC, but that may be too late to enable to complete the Chamera project by December, 1992. NPHC officials said the dam had been designed keeping in mind the fact that the area fell in the seeond worst earthquake - prone zone in the country. It would withstand tremors to the level of six on the Richter scale. The project comprises three units of 180 MW each and power generated from it would be transmitted to the northern regional grid at Moga.

For this, a 236-KM-long transmission line is envisaged while the system comprises a 400 KV double circuit twin conductor. The project is partly financed by Export Development Corporation and the Canadian International Development Agency (CIDA) for import of construction machinery while consultancy services are provided by SNCACRES of Canada. As per the clearance of the Public Investment Board (PIB) in 1983 the project was to be completed in March 1990.

However, NHPC officials said nearly three years were lost as the agreement with CIDA was signed the project were delayed in forest clearance, floods and geological surprises during excavation. The land acquired for the Chamera project totals 1344 hectares of which 1075 hectares come under reservoir submergence area. A virtual township has sprung up in the victinity of the project with large number of temporary and parament quarters being built. A fallout of the project has been the spiralling of real estate prices in picturesque Delhousie and nearby the Chamera project would be Punjab, Haryana, Jammu and Kashmir and Himachal Pradesh.

An important component of the project is the intricate system of tunnels blasted through the adjoining mountain range during which technicians came across the phenomenon of "squeezing". This means that once a tunnel is blasted or portions of it excavated, the rocks above exert pressure on the griders put up to maintain the required diametre. Due to the natural pressure of the rock, the griders get twisted and the diametre of the tunned is reduced. This phenomenon was experienced in a 400-metre stretch of which water would be transported. The rock pressure had subsided and stabilised within two in the 105 MW. Loktak project in Manipur offered the geological surprises and also contributed to the hurdles caused by the "squeezing."

Once the water passes through the turbines in the power house generating electricity, it would flow back into River Ravi through a 2445 metre long tailrace tunnel. This tunnel passes below the river bed and finally meets the river. Both the power and tailrace tunnels are horse-shoe shaped. In each phase of the 1,743 crore project, work is at an advanced stage, according to the general manager, Mr Nagbhushan. Project officials claim that the morale among the workforce was high and there was no reason to delay the commissioning of the project beyond December next year. Efforts to secure loans from banks and public institutions have not met with an encouraging response. The NHPC had also not succeeded in raising anything through bonds. It will, however, get Rs. 50 crore from LIC at the rate of 17.5 per cent interest.

Nuclear Power

The target for nuclear power production has been scaled down only by 1,000 megawatt (MW) from 10,000 set for 2000 A.D. "We had to reduce the target due to the financial crunch as the allocation is likely to be only Rs. 16,000 crore against the original demand of Rs. 32,000 crore to produce 10,000 MW by 2000 A.D." Dr. R.P.K. Iyenger chairman, Atomic Energy Commission said on August 26, 1991. Dr Iyenger reiterated that revised target for 2,000 A.D. was generation of merely 7,000 mw from pressurised heavy water reactors (PHWR), and 2000 MW from light water reactors likely to be commissioned with the Soviet help. However, the latest annual report of the Development of Atomic Energy (DAE) has a different story to tell. The report indicates that only 6,050 MW of power is estimated to be produced from nuclear reactor by the end of this decade. This figure has been arrived at taking into account the existing capacity and the future projects nearing completion. The country has an installed capacity of 1,456 MW from seven nuclear plants—two each at Tarapur, Rajasthan, Kalpakkam and a 235 MW unit at Narora.

Even more projects are likely to be ready in the next four years. These are: one 235 MW unit at Narora (by August end, 1991) two 235 MW units at Kakrapara in Gujarat (one by December 1991 and the other by December 1992), two units of 235 MW each at Rajasthan and Kaiga, Karnataka by 1995 These seven units total 1,645 MW. If four more 235 MW units (220 Mw unit each) planned at Kaiga and the two 1,000 MW

Soviet reactors likely to be commissioned at Koodan Kulam, Tamil Nadu are taken into account, the total installed capacity will be 6050 MW. The political developments in the Soviet Union have put a question mark over the two LWRs to be installed at koodankulam. Dr. Iyengar's assertion is also based on the assumption that six 500 MW units (four at Rajasthan and two at Tarapur) proposed to be set up by the end of this decade will be ready. However, DAE sources said the engineering design of these units is still in progress. So far only the financial sanction is over and the site selection has been completed.

The ministry of environment has not yet cleared the four units at Kaiga and the two 500 MW units at Rawatbhata, Rajasthan. It takes nearly eight years to build one reactor if everything is right but all the existing units took more than 10 years to commissions. The first Kakrapara unit, if ready on its target date of December 1992, would have taken eight years. It is not all bleak for the nuclear sector. Dr Iyengar said the country's offer to build research reactors abroad has met with encouraging response. Egypt and Syria may opt or 5 MW Indian-built research reactors. Queries from a few other countries have also been received. "When we entered the nuclear field in the fifties, we had the benefit of training at small research reactors in the US. But these facilities do not exist now. There is a demand for small research reactor and we have the expertise to build them", Dr. Iyengar noted.

Earlier Dr. Iyengar said the relevance of small and medium sized (200 to 600 MW) reactors is far greater as compared to a few years back. It is important that new reactor designs which answer some of the important issues relating to nuclear safety directly rather than through backfit or modification, were evolved and nuclear power development is put on a move firmer footing. India has consistently adopted small reactors due to considerations such as size of electricity distribution grids advantage of repeating a design, lower capital investment and greater possibility of indigenisation of power plants.

Chapter IV

State Government Should Reform

Unless some ways are found to reform the State Governments' financial excesses, much of India's economy will continue to be in a mess. Many of the worst financial excesses of the past decades have been indulged in by the states and not by the central government. For the vast majority of our people, the State Government matters much more than the centre.

When the Indian version of federation was originally devised, it envisaged a clear distinction between the sources of revenue for the centre and the states. The basis of the division of fiscal powers enshrined in the constitution was quite simply that all taxes which would have an inter-state base would be levied by the centre, while those with a local base would be levied by the states.

In addition, there would be some taxes that, though collected by the centre, would be given wholly or partially to the states. In order to correct any fiscal imbalance between the revenues of the various states, arising out of the difference caused by element like the population and the level of industrialisation between states, the states were to receive grants-in-aid from the centre, which would further increased the level of transfers between the two levels of government. Over and above this, there were the loans, given to the states to meet their various revenue expenditures.

Slowly with the passage of time, the contribution of the centre to the overall financial resources of the states has increased dramatically. In 1951-52, just 25 per cent of the state expenditure was met by the centre, but by the end of the Seventh plan, this figure rose to a high 48.2 per cent. According to statistics from the Reserve Bank of India, while the gross transfer of resources, compromising the states' share in the various duties and taxes, were budgeted at Rs. 39.312 crore in

1990-91, the total plan and non-plan loans for 1990-91 were budgeted at Rs. 12,226.7 crore. More often than not, this money has been spent on the in-efficiently run state Electricity Boards, the Transport Corporations, Irrigation Works and the like. But what has actually increased the spending of the states has been the game played by the dishonest and corrupt politicians with the assistance of willing bureaucracy.

The percentage of central spending on the state has gone up tremendously over the years. In 1951-52, the states' percentage of the central spending was 22.1 per cent, while in 1989-90, it had risen to a whopping 44.1 per cent at Rs. 31.085 crore. This excessive spending has thus led to a persistent trend of imbalances, being reflected in the finance of the states, over the years. The gap between the receipts and expenditures has been widening, as reflected in the higher budget deficit of the states. The collective deficit of all the states was Rs. 961.2 crore in 1989-90.

This revenue deficit was the result of a higher growth in revenue expenditures, by 3.7 per cent, which far exceeded the growth of 2.1 per cent in the revenue receipts. What is most disquieting is that in the pressure on the state government finance, has been on account of the unsustainable growth in non- developmental expenditures and the sharp deterioration in the financial results of the state public enterprises. The lack of determined efforts at mobilising resources, on the part of the states, also plays its part. Non-development expenditures today account for over a quarter of the state budget. It was budgeted at Rs. 24,285.3 crore for 1990-91. This budgeted estimate represents a rise of 22.6 per cent over 1989-90. That year itself, non-developmental expenditure registered a rise of 24.7 per cent over 1988-89. Of the total non-developmental expenditure, the interest payments on the loans taken by the states from the national exchequer, and the appropriations to reserve, for the reduction of debt, alone account for 39.6 per cent in 1990-91, while the administrative services account for 34.4 per cent non-developmental non-plan expenditure in fact, had accounted for 98 per cent of the total non-developmental expenditure in the Seventh plan.

The Ninth Finance Commission (NFC) headed by N.K.P. Salve had estimated the outstanding debt of the states at the end of March 1989 at Rs. 79,640 crore, as compared to Rs. 18,780 crore in March 1979. The most glaring feature of the states' debt is that over 70 per cent of this is owed to the Centre.

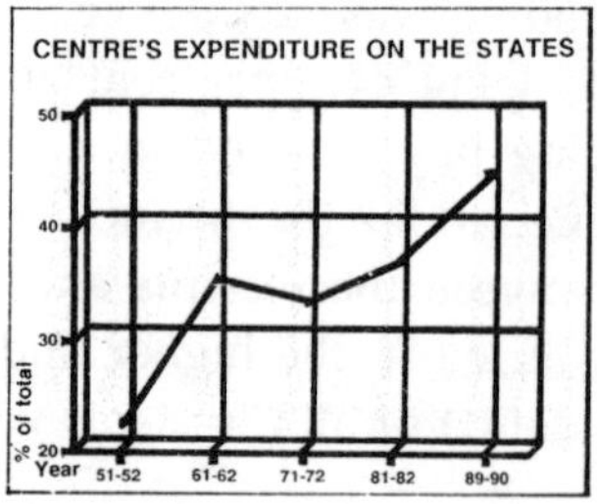

Source : The Illustrated Weekly of India, July 27-August 2, 1991.

The Centre has lifted many control on the setting up of new industries under the New Industrial Policy of August 1991. However, even if a businessman no longer needs an industrial licence or MRTP clearance, he still has to go to the state governments for clearance or location, for getting water and power connections, for fixing the percentage of workers he can employ who do not belong to the state, and for vitually all laws pertaining to retirement and closure. The industrialist cannot shift his plant without the state government's permission or sell his land and building without the approval of the state government. The centre may have opened up most areas to private investment but many state governments still want monopoly control over transport corporations, power distribution under the state controlled State Electricity Board, water distribution, local roads, and a host of items that matter most to local people.

The state government's controls constitute one gigantic racket that enable politicians to make unearned money and weave a web of patronage. They have utter contempt for financial or any other sort of public accountability. According to a senior civil servant in Lucknow, ministers simply dip their hand straight into the treasury and help themselves to cash and the bureaucracy is so crushed and cynical that it colludes instead of protesting. Dozens of state corporations have not finalised their accounts for years on end, and nobody knows how much cash has been embezzled and by whom.

The National Development Council meeting initiated effective measures to reduce the growing administrative expenditure of states to ensure that fiscal deficit could be kept within a certain limit during the Eighth plan (1992-97). At the meeting of the Parliamentary Consultative Committee attached to the Ministry of Planning and Programme Implementation, the members were informed on November 25, 1991 that revenue collection by states had lagged behind the estimate made by the Planning Commission and the Finance Commission, while their non-development expenditure was on the rise.

The Planning Commission proposed to emphasise on the need for accelerating development exenditure and reducing non-development expenditure, particularly the spending on administration. The Eighth Plan was being formulated in the background of a mix of circumtances, including the recent policy reforms initiated by the government to revitalise the economy.

Inefficient Performance

However, much has been written about the poor performance of the central public sector undertakings, but at least it makes a profit of something like Rs. 3,000 crore a year. By contrast, the State Electricity Boards and Road Transport Corporations lose more than Rs. 5,000 crore a year. The magnitude of losses in the state corporations may be less, but these are replete with most bizare stories of waste and sloth. According to Dr. Ashok Guha, the West Bengal government set up a dairy corporation decade ago with 20,000 cows and 1,000 employees. As the years went by the cows died but the employees multiplied. Eventually, there were 5,000 cows and 5,000 employees. In effect, the state government was paying these employees to drink the little milk they produced.

Meanwhile, Rs. 596 crore were spent on Haldia Fertiliser to produce nothing. The comptroller and auditor-general of India (CAG) has indicted the Hindustan Fertiliser Corporation Limited (HFC) for the delay in Haldia Fertiliser project which has remained "unproductive so far" even after a massive investment of Rs. 596 crore. In his report in Haldia Fertiliser Project of HFC laid in Parliament on September 4,1991, the CAG said besides the mammoth investment which remained in frustuous standing of charges of over Rs. 1.50 crore per annum were being incurred by the corporation separately. The report said due to various design deficiencies, technical problems, mismatching of equipment, time and cost over runs. The project cost zoomed from Rs. 88.03 crore to over Rs. 596 crore by March 1990. The very purpose for which the project was set up i.e. to meet the increased demand in Eastern region of India for phosphatic and nitrogenous fertiliser remained unfulfilled.

Similar stories can be multiplied in all state corporations. Dr. Manmohan Singh, the Union Finance Minsiter may talk about the importance of living within one's means, but State Electricity Boards have long stopped paying Coal India LTD and Bharat Heavy Electricals Ltd for supplies of coal and machinery. Some discipline is being enforced here by deducting advance plan assistance to the states and transferring it to the creditors, but this is a political act and not a market approach. The concrete solution is to give every supplier, including those in the public sector undertakings, a free hand to stop supplier to all defaulters. That alone will instil a sense of discipline and accountability in state governments. Deducting plan assistance creates a centre-state dispute, which is the wrong way of approaching what should be seen as commercial discipline. Only such a discipline will make state government to pay more attention to collecting electricity dues and stopping the theft of power.

Another way of bringing about accountability would be to bring the public sector units, within the purview of the MRTP Act. Right now, a state government can totally ignore the needs of customers while operating monopolies in roads, canals, checking dams and a look of the other matters. To a fair extent this is also true of the central public sector undertakings. If a state government .cannot operate bus service efficiently, why should the public be deprived of services that private operaters can offer ? Why should not villages have the right to build dams and local roads on their own? Why should private operaters not be allowed to operate tourism services on the same terms as state corporations ? Where the centre and states can justify a restrictive practices to the MRTP commission they may be allowed to continue, but not otherwise. All public sector undertakings should be toned up for their functioning especially in the light of the recent economic and fiscal measures. They should evolve "innovative steps" for improving productivity and raising resource for modernisation and upgradation of technology. One of the "buring problems" of the public sector undertaking is foreign exchange crunch. The public sector undertakings would now have to compete in the open markets for producing foreign exchange through the purchases of REP licence and Exim crips. This would jeopordise the production line of many major public sector undertakings. The recent depreciation of rupee had also badly affected the public sector undertakings (PSUs). Some mechanisrm would have to be evolved in order to ensure the PSUs were also able to meet the booked orders abroad without much hardship. An effort should be made on maintaining harmonious industrial relations among PSUs and hence every effort would be made to protect the interest of the workers.

Radical Changes in MRTP Act

According to the World Bank Report,[1] the MRTP Act has not been particularly effective in attaining its main objectives

---

1. The World Bank Reports - India, an industrialising Economy in transition (1990).

to curb the concentration of economic power, to prevent restrictive competitive practices and to control unfair trade practices because of its focus on asset size and market shares. In fact, it has sometimes, restricted competition rather stimulated it. It is suggested that MRTP board be set up for surveillance of anti-competitive and anti-consumer behaviour that the code of unfair practice be further developed and its penalties strengthened. The interference of the government through MRTP Act in investment decision of large corporations has become deleterious in its effects of Indian industrial growth. The pre-entry scrutiny of investment decision by the so-called MRTP companies will no longer be required. The thrust of the policy will be more on controlling unfair and restrictive business practices. The MRTP Act has been amended to remove the threshold limits of assets in respective of MRTP companies and dominant undertakings. This eliminates the requirement of prior approval of central government investment subsidies and the use of licensing to direct industries to backward areas could be replaced by direct production subsidies on concession of excise and sales tax.

Appropriate incentives and the design of investment in infrastructural development will be used to promote the dispersal of industry particularly to rural areas and backward areas to reduce congestion in cities. The public sector undertakings should progressively be required to compete on a more equal basis with private sector producers and importers. Overtime, this would involve the phased removal of purchasing and price preference and protection from competition through controlled marketing arrangements Portfolio of public sector investments will be reviewed with a view to focussing the public sector on strategic, high tech and essential infrustructure. Whereas some reservation for the public sector is being retained there would be no bar for exclusive areas to be opened up to the private sector selectively. Competition will also be induced in these areas by inviting private sector participation.

The new Industrial Policy is certainly an important improvement in the world Bank report on certain aspects. What could have prompted Dr. Manmohan Singh, the Union Finance Minister, to go in for measures more drastic than those suggested by the World Bank. The only significant thing that happened during the interrequum between the publication of the World Bank report and the New Industrial Policy is that the government approached IMF, the sister organisation of the World Bank for a loan to tide over its extremely serious foreign exchange crisis. The IMF policy prescriptions were never published. They remained confidential to common people.

The President of India promulgated an ordinance on September 27,1991 making radical change in the Monopolies and Restrictive Trade Practices (MRTP) Act. The Ordinance, though in tune with the new Industrial Policy is a surprise coming as it does just 10 days after the budget session of Parliament ended. Companies with assets worth more than Rs. 100 crore will not any more have to be registered under the MRTP Act and as such will not have to take the Centre's permission for expansion, establishment of new undertakings, merger, amalgamation, take-over or appointment of directors. The ordinance instead gives more powers to the MRTP commission to control and regulate monopolistic, restrictive and unfair trade practices.

These changes have been made because the government has realised that "per-entry restriction under the MRTP Act on the investment decision of the corporate sector has outlived its utility and has become a hindrance to the speedy implementation of industrial projects." said the Minsiter of State for law, Mr. Rangarajan Kumaramangalam who further pointed out that the pre- entry restriction could be imposed in barely five per cent of the cases and had failed to check concentration of wealth.

The government also issued a notification extending the ambit of the MRTP Act to public sector undertakings, financial institutions and cooperative societies. The notification, however, exempts undertakings related to defence, atomic energy and currency from the purview of the Act. This is because they involve state secrets, when asked why the government had instead not introduced a Bill in Parliament in this regard, Mr.

Kumaramangalam claimed that the omission was entirely because of a personal reason, "since, I also handle parliamentary affairs, I did not want other ministers to feel that I was pushing my bill at the expense of theirs in the short time that was available", he said.

Under the new scheme of things, the MRTP Commission is expected to handle greater volume of cases and the government is, therefore, in the process of agumenting its staff and infrastructure. The government was seriously considering the prospect of opening "benches" of the commission in all the state capitals. The bulk of the cases before the MRTP Commission relate to unfair trade practices that is promotion of goods and services by making false claims about their quality and performances. The ordinance has enlarged the definition of unfair trade practices to include false representation about the quality of goods as well. More importantly, a consumer now does not have to prove his personal loss to make a complaint.

If its orders are not obeyed, the commission has always had the power to launch prosecution against the errant company before a criminal court. But the penalty for unfair trade practices under the earlier provision was only imprisonment upto three years or fine upto Rs. 10,000 or both. the ordinance has made the fine compulsary and enhanced the upper limit to Rs. 10 lakh. It has also stipulated that the imprisonment will be for at least six months.

The sanctions for monopolistic trade practices (formation of a cartel to maintain unreasonable high prices) and restrictive trade practices to maintain unreasonably (prevention of competition) have been similarly made stiffer. At the same time, the ordinance empowers the commission to compound offence relating to the contravention of its orders either before or after launching prosecution. With the deletion of clauses related to pre-entry restrictions, all the pending applications under those provisions will be treated as closed and the undertakings concerned can now proceed with their projects without any MRTP clearance.

Chapter V

New Industrial Policy : Public and Private Sector

Who drafted the Narashimha Rao Government's Industrial Policy ? The Indian bureaucracy, World Bank or the IMF ? Both the Prime Minister and Finance Minsiter are on record as saying that the industrial policy has not been dictated or even influenced by the World Bank or the IMF. If this claim is to be believed, then it will appear that the World Bank lifted a number of points from the government's industrial policy long before it was finalised. The World Bank report has not only structural similarities with the industrial policy but at places, the ideas are exactly the same.

According to the World Bank report, the licensing system has discouraged potential investors, dampened the overall growth of industrial investment and inhibited the ability of firms to take advantage of economies of scale...It is accordingly suggested that all forms of capacity licensing for industry could be phased out completely over the medium term...A list could be prepared of those few industries which pose security, health, safety or environmental concerns for which special permit would be required from the Central Government.Weapons, explosives and nuclear energy are examples of industries that might require such a permit.

The winds of change have been with India for some time and the industrial licensing system has been graduallly moving away from the concept of capacity licensing. Further impetus must be provided to these change which along can push the country towards the attainment of its entrepreneurial and industrial potential and this calls for bold and imaginative decisions destined to remove restraints on capacity... industrial licensing will be abolished for all projects, except for a short list of industries related to security and strategic concerns, social reasons, hazardous chemicals and overriding environmental reasons. Appropriate incentive and the design of investment in infrastructure development will be used to promote the disposal of industry particularly to rural areas and backward areas and to reduce congestion in cities.

July 24, 1991, may be termed as a red letter day in this connection for on this day the Government of India announced a major policy reform for industrial development in the form of a new industrial policy synchronising it with a trade policy reform and the 1991-92 budget exercise, but keeping close to the original act of 1951 on the main inspiration. The making of the policing has not been as sudden as its announcement. The new policy responds, in a very large measure, to a genuine need of the producing industry, the consuming sector and the investor. Its importance is to be seen not so much in its visible content valuable as it is as in the welcome psychology of government approach to industrialisation and in the hard nosed recognition of the need for government's self-effacement of its Big Brother image.

The policy sincerely aims at mitigating the more serious constraints faced by the Indian and the foreign investor. It provides for the first time, freedom to the industry to chart out its own course of growth in terms of production capacity, diversification, modernisation, management and international orientation.

Monopoly tags fixing monetary ceilings for growth of private enterprises have been removed and MRTP Act it has been appropriatly amended. Locational embargoes have been lifted so that industrial projects may be set up anywhere purely on the rationale of commercial factors of establishment and operation and economic and environmental parameters of plant location. The industry is considerably lightened of its burden of excessive bureaucratic attention. The new policy has generally been hailed as a bold attempt at industrial reform. In short, the unbinding of long-suffering prometheus has begun. perhaps for the first time in India's history of industrialisation, private sector industry's progress is, in a sense, a matter of its own concern and responsibility. The onus to perform or perish is on it. The new policy represents a major breakthrough from the past or as Time magazine picture squarely put it, "a cloudburst."

According to the New Policy

Eight(8) Areas (Defence equipment; Atomic energy; related minerals; coal and lignite; mineral oils; Mining of iron, managanese and chrome ores, gypsum, sulphur, gold and diamond; Mining of copper, lead, zinc, tin, molydenum and wolfram; railway transport) only are reserved for the public sector.

—The system of industrial licensing is dispensed with except for 18 specified industries.

—Reservation of items for the small scale sector will continue.

—Existing and new industrial projects and free to broadband their range of production if no additional investment in plant and machinery is involved.

—Substantial expansion schemes of existing industrial units are exempt from licensing.

—DGID registrations of schemes dispensed with.

Foreign Investment and Collaboration

—Automatic approval of direct foreign investment upto 51 per cent equity in 34 years.

—Companies with 51 per cent foreign equity encouraged to act as trading houses primarily engaged in export business.

—Foreign equity proposals need not necessarily be accompanied by foreign technology agreement.

—A special empowered Board will be set up in the government to negotiate with international firms and approve direct foreign investment in select areas.

—Automatic permission for foreign technology agreements in high priority industries for a lumpsum payment of upto Rs. 10 milllion, Royalty 5 percent on domestic and 8 per cent on exports subject to a total payment of 8 per cent of sales over a 10 year period from the date of agreement or 7 years from the commencement of production.

—Automatic permission, subject to the same guidelines, as above, to industries other than those in the list of high priority areas if no free foreign exchange is required for any payments.

—No permission needed for hiring foreign technicians or foreign testing of indigenously developed products.

Import of Capital Goods

—Automatic clearance for import of capital goods if the foreign exchange requirement for such imports is ensured through foreign equity.

—Automatic approval for import of capital goods if C.I.F. value of the capital goods to be imported is less than 25 per cent of the total value of plant and machinery subject to a maximum limit of Rs. 20 million.

Project Loan Capital

—Mandatory convertibility clause which enabled financial institutions to convert loans into equity has been dispensed with.

Every silver lining has a cloud. A segment of the large scale sector perhaps wishes for the inclusion or non-inclusion of some industries for which the industrial licensing system will still continue; and for the inclusion or non-inclusion of some industries in the list of industries which have 51 per cent foreign equity participation rights and automatic approval under certain conditions. The continuance of the system of price and distribution control of some industries is also considered as a deterrant by it. The small and medium scale sector has cause to be jubilant as it has a larger scope for horizontal and vertical growth, especially under the facility of automatic approval of import of capital goods upto 25 per cent of the total value of plant and machinery subject to a ceiling of Rs. 20 million. A separate reform policy for the small scale sector is also on the anvil.

Reforms, in their very nature, tend to refine and improve themselves in the light of experience. It is reasonable to believe that with an earnest effort at its implementation, the new policy can only lead to a better industrial future.

Nevertheless, the new industrial policy is certainly an improvement on the World Bank report in certain aspects. The "freedom" is the price having demanded liberasation of the Indian economy and having got it, the private sector will now have to shoulder its responsibilities. Indian industry has grown accustomed to a system of controls and supports that are no longer available under the new economic policy. This will create certain "teething problems", but industry will have to learn to adopt and adjust to the new situation. The Planning Commission is preparing to off load some of the responsibilities pertaining to infrastructure on the the private sector. The Planning Commission, will from now on prepare only indicative plans on the basis of available resources.

At the same time, the planning commission is committed to exploring alternative source of energy as the coutry's reserve of hydrocarbons is not abundant and imports are expensive. The Planning Commission will try and bring about a balance between thermal and hydel sources of electricity in the Eighth Plan. Modernisation does not mean reduction of labour force. The government has announced an *exit policy* for inefficient industrial units. Modernisation does not necessarily mean rationalisation of the labour force. It also means efficient use of energy and improvement in the quality of goods and services. The move for global integration of the Indian economy was difficult under the existing rule and regulations that circumstribed the industrial sector. Indeed, the corporate sector has started consolidating its position, in a bid to face the onslaught of competition expected from the multinationals in the country. Tie-ups with existing collaborators are being extended and re-examined in the changed environment. The hunt for new partners has also begun in right earnest. The export base of the country has to be widened to include hi-tech items.

Foreign Equity Holding Raised to 51 per cent

The government of India on November 19,1991 announced the guideline for automatic approval to existing companies with foreign shares holding to increase this state to 51 per cent. Companies exclusively engaged in high priority industries (these industries where the new industrial policy has provided for foreign equity holding of 51 per cent) can increase the exciting foreign share-holding of 51 per cent and other companies can also do this provided their expansion programmes are for the specified high priority industries. In both cases, the additional foreign equity must be remitted into the country in foreign exchange. The industry ministry has also announced details of the procedures for increasing foreign equity preferential share allocation and share valuation in the case of foreign investors.

The new industrial policy statement made by the government on July 24,1991 had allowed automatic approval of investment proposals with foreign equity holding upto 51 per cent in specified high priority industries. Following this, there was a demand for a clear-cut set of guidelines for automaticity in approval of proposals by existing companies with foreign shareholding to raise their equity to 51 per cent. Under the provisions of FERA, the government has asked foreign companies to dilute their share-holding to less than 40 per cent in the early 1970s.

Referring to the requirement of preferential Share allocation, the announcement said, on receipt of the Reserve Bank of India approved the company not pass a special resolution under section 81(1A) of the Companies Act proposing preferential allocation of the required volume of fresh equity to the foreign investor. In respect of the equity holdings of the financial institutions in such companies, the Finance Ministry will seperately advise the institutions that they may support such proposals provided in their commercial Judgement, they are in the interest of the company.

The Controller of Capital Issue (CCI) will allow preferential allocation of equity in favour of the foreign investor on the basis of the Reserve Bank approval for expansion of equity and the adoption of the special resolution by the company. In such cases, the price of new equity will be fixed by CCI on the basis of market prices with a discount of upto 10 per cent. In the case of import of capital goods for expansion programmes, the Reserve Bank will have to confirm whether the import is covered by foreign equity. Based on this, CCI will issue the relevant import licence. Under this provision, plant and machinery which will be imported should be new and not second hand. The Reserve Bank will also monitor the outflow of foreign exchange in the form of dividend payments which are to be balanced by export earnings.

New Trade Policy

The following were the highlights of the 13-point major trade reforms announced by the government of India on July 4, 1991:

1. Cash Compensatory Scheme (CCS) suspended with effect from July 3,1991. All imports actually effected until the mid- night of July 2-3, 1991, will honour, be entitled to the benefits of CCS.

2. Replenishment Licencing Scheme (REP) to become the principal instrument for export-related imports. It will now be called exim scrip and can be freely traded.

3. All exports to have a uniform REP rate of 30 per cent of the freight on board (FOB) value from the present rate ranging from 5 to 20 per cent of the FOB value. Special rates for gems and jewellery, certain metal-based handicrafts and books and magazine will, however, continue.

4. The new REP scheme to give maximum incentive to exporters where import intensity is low like agricultural exports.
5. All supplementary licences stand abolished except in the case of the small scale sector and for producers of life-saving drugs/equipment. These two categories would be entitled to import both under Open General Licences (OGL) or through supplementary licences.
6. All additional licences granted to export houses stand abolished. However, they will enjoy a REP rate of 30 per cent of FOB value and will be granted an additional REP of 5 per cent of FOB value.
7. All items which figure in lists like the limited permissable list now to be imported through the REP route.
8. Unlimited OGL contained in the Exim policy stands abolished and all items under this category to be imported only through the REP scheme.
9. Advance licensing for obtaining imports for exporters will remain open. However, the REP rate for advance licence exports is being increased from 10 per cent of net foreign exchange (NFE) to 20 per cent of NFE.
10. All import licensing for capital goods and rew materials except for a small "negative list" to be removed in three years.
11. All items to be decanalised except that are essential and major changes in the entire canalisation policy to be announced shortly.
12. Financial institutions would also be allowed to trade in Exim Scrips. In due course, the Exim scrips to be replaced with foreign exchange certificates which will be more easily tradable.
13. The rupee is expected to be fully convertible on the trade account in three to five years.

In this 13-point decontrol package for trade, the trade policy had been liberalised and overhauled as on July 3, 1991. Sweeping changes abolished the cash compensatory scheme (CCS) for exporters as well as all licensing for capital goods and raw materials. Almost all imports would now be under an expanded replenishment route though REP licence would now be called Exim scrips - 30 per cent of exports - and these being freely traded. However, petroleum, fertiliser and edible oil remained protected.

The adminsitrative controls had so far stipled enterprise and "spawned arbitrariness". The system of using discretion had caused delays, waste, inefficiency and corruption. The trade policy had now been left to the normal market process instead of bureaucratic whims. The CCS became redundant. However, small scale industry and life saving drugs would not be affected and advance licensing would continue to be studied on a case-to-case basis for exporters who still do not wish to use Exim scrips.

A category of unlisted Open-General Licence had been abolished as had supplementary licences under which imports of Rs. 2,000 to Rs. 3,000 crore were permitted. The CCS cost the exchequer Rs. 2,000 crore a year. This subsidy would be a net saving for the national development. Except for essential imports through the State Trading Corporation (STC) and other agencies, all imports had been decanalised. Once all licensing was removed for capital goods and raw materials, one should be able to import one's requirements by paying rupees.

The replenishment of exports would be the principal instrument. The uniform replenishment rate of 30 per cent was up from the present 5 to 20 per cent of FOB value. These were special rates for gems and jewellery. Rate for agricultural exports were up from 5 to 30 per cent to help them make gains from open trading. To make this system more "transparent and free" the government proposed that financial institutions might also be allowed to trade in Exim Scrips (REP); the details were being worked out.

Mr. P. Chidambaram, the Union State Minister for Commerce expected the trade deficit in dollar terms to be less in 1990-91 and hoped by the end of the year 1991-92 a 9 per cent growth would be achieved. Summing up, he said an opportunity was being given to the exporters who had been wanting it for many years: "We have wings, yet we have been daunted by the fears of flying. Let us now soar into the high skies," the Commerce Minister stated rhetorically. He promised industry and trade the bull support of the government in this great effort.

Mixed Reaction from Industry

Mr. S.K. Birla, Persident of the Federation of Indian Chambers of Commerce and Industry (FICCI) welcomed the policy announcement made by the Union Minister of State for Commerce: "It is a bold and imaginative step. It seems to be a major move towards restructuring the economy and particularly international trade."

Mr. Birla commended the decision to introduce a uniform 30 per cent REP rates which would reduce the procedural delays and paper work. The new scheme would locate a direct motivation for larger exports particularly of those items whose import- intensity is low. However, a system will have to be evolved to expedite issue of Exim scrips. In fact, these shall be made automatic on receipt of remittance by banks. He also pointed out that over a period of time, at the full maturity of the scheme, the REP rate should be enhanced from the present 30 to 60 per cent and more imports should be placed under its ambit to cater to the needs of all industries.

He thought it was necessary to continue canalisation of steel, non-ferrous metals and feed block for fertilisers for which there was not enough indigenous supply and which had to be imported in bulk. Mr. Birla also appreciated the efforts of the government to lift import curbs as also to review the tariff structure. This was imperative against the backdrop of the steep depreciation of the rupee by 20 per cent.

Mr. S.S. Bhasin, Chairman Engineering Export Promotion Council expressed shock at the decision taken by the government to completely withdraw CCS on engineering products in respect of export shipments from July 3, 1991. He pointed out that such an abrupt withdrawal of a scheme, which was the backbone for development of exports of not only engineering but the whole lot of manufactured goods from India, totally had shaken the confidence of exporting community. Mr. Bhasin thought no consideration had been given to the negative impact of depreciation in rupee value on overall export realisation, because of increased cost of imported input going into export production, likely spurt in labour costs arising from general inflation, jumps in shipping freight price and international price of steel and pig iron would narrow down, and so on.

Mr. L.K. Modi, President, North Indian Chamber of Commerce and Industry urged adequate and timely availability of liberal export finances to small scale units for boosting exports. The suggestion of the NICCI president assumed importance against the backdrop of severe problems being faced by small-scale exporters to avail export finance from banking sector primarily due to the curbs introduced by the RBI on credit lending. This, in many cases, he said, has affected execution of export orders by the small scale sectors which already bagged the orders worth crores of rupees despite international competition. Export orders, worth several crores of rupees were being locked up due to the inflexible stand taken by the banking sector in extending export finance to SSIS at the instance of the RBI.

The non-performance of the export orders of those units would put the Indian firms in a very bad light and would be very difficult for them to bag orders in future. Therefore, it was suggested that the RBI should follow a liberal finance policy by extending the finance by examining the merit of each case till the time the credit curbs were lifted up completely.

Confederation of Engineering Industry (CEI) commended the introduction of the Exim Scrip concept, to be replaced later by foreign exchange certificates in place of REP licences. The uniform rate of 30 per cent also brought in major rationalisation. However, the engineering industry whose REP licence rates were between 15 and 20 per cent benefit the least, though their own import requirements in terms of raw materials, components and capital goods were essential and significant. The CEI also appreciated the retention of the advance licensing scheme, which provided duty free imports against export orders. What was important was to ensure swiftness in the issue of advance licenses preferably withing 15 days of application by exporters.

Free Trade

The Union Commerce Minsiter, Mr. P. Chidambaram said on December 29, 1991 that all licences and controls of trade would go by March-end, 1992. Speaking at an NRI international Seminar in Hyderabad, Mr. Chidambaram said already 90 per cent of the controls and licences had gone and the remaining would go latest by March-end, 1992. This would enable more capital inflow from the non-resident Indians and to generate momentum to development of Indian economy.

He also listed out various concessions and subsidies announced by the Centre to attract foreign capital and enable NRIs to set up industries and invest their money in India. Any proposal by an NRI to set up a unit anywere in India would be treated on priority basis and delays and procedural complexity had been cut drastically by the "automatic approval" scheme, applicable to 34 types of industries. Next year the list would be enlarged by including more and more industries, he said, and called upon the NRIs to invest in India in the business of their choice and convenience.

The Central Government, headed by Mr. P.V. Narasimha Rao is committed to keep economic agenda on the centre stage, which would alone bring development to the country. He also criticised the previous non-Congress governments in the Centre for their "wrong economic policies" and "independence towards real development. Even when the present government came to power the country's credit worthiness was very low. Only with the bold and sincere decisions taken by the Prime Minister was the global confidence in our country restored. The reserves which were Rs. 6,000 crores when the persent government came to power had risen to Rs. 9,500 crores now which was a remarkable achievement. On two occasions earlier, in 1971 and 1984, India had conceded international market to China and some Latin American countries, due to the wrong policies of the then non-Congress governments. Provided the political willingness could be mustered to allow sick units to be phased out of the system, the proposed national renewal fund - already planned by the Government of India - could be the source of credits for creating a social safety net and for compensating and retraining laid off workers.

India's economy did not allow any exit policy whatsoever all these years, whether in the private or in the public sector. That approach would have to change. The Bank would help with funds that would be over and above the finance available annually from the Aid India Consortium, the Bank authorities added. The Bank was also "keenly hoping to see" some meaningful reforms in India's financial sector. Whether bank would be privatised was not the issue, as long as their functioning allowed them to become competitive and a level playing field was provided for all competitors, new and old in the financial sector. However, the World Bank had off-repeated complaint against mismanagement in India's power sector.

It seemed that an exit policy had become invitable and it was incumbent on the government to seek the fullest co-operation of trade unions in formulating a policy that would minimise their resistance. Unfortunately, the government has faltered. For instance, the decision to set up a tripartite committee, comprising representatives of trade unions, employers in the private sector and the government to discuss policies and issues concerning workers, was taken on August 17,1991. But for some inexplicable reason the committee was formed as late as mid-November, 1991. The emerging confrontation between the Centre and trade unions on the formulation of an "exit policy" points to the government's failure to address the apprehensions of labour stemming from sweeping change in economic policy. The government must have been aware when it embarked on these changes in June, 1991 that a revamp of the public sector as well as competitive pressure unleashed by new industrial policy would eventually lead to closure of unviable and inefficient units and retrenchment of labour. It was necessary, therefore, to explore ways and means to make this adjustment for labour as painless as possible. In fact, Dr. Manmohan Singh, recognised the importance of the problem when he announced the proposal for a National Renewal Fund in his budget speech on July 24, 1991.

The World Bank was ready to provide substantial finance to help India implement an exit policy for unviable industrial units and to create a social safety net. The amount for US $ 500 million was available from savings on past IDA credits to India because of surplus fund generated by Indian devaluation and other causes. Normally these funds would revert to IDA.

The World Bank could arrange around half a billion dollars for starting such a "national renewal fund". From internal resources India could generate more money for the fund until some bilateral donors could be perscuaded to chip in as well.

Without an exit policy, through which sick or otherwise unviable units would be allowed to die, India's recently launched economic reform programme would not succeed to the extent necessary. This raises a number of questions. How is the government to decide which enterprises are totally unviable, as distinct from borderline case where small infusions of capital or new equipment could revive them? Is there any criteria other than profitability that ought to be applied? What happens to employee of the enterprise to be liquidated ? Who decides on the mode of liquidation and on the choice between outright closure, sale or a takeover by employees? What are the possibilities of worker's co-operatives in some cases?

It is that the human costs of nationalisation and closure of any undertaking must be minimised as far as possible and that workers ought to be retained so that they can be absorbed in other industries on a priority basis.

This agreement is rooted not merely in the imperative of social policy but in the compulsion of political survival in a democracy as complex as India's. This is not to argue that the economy should not move firmly towards a strong, vibrant, viable public sector, banish white elephants and shed inefficiency. The IMF is interested in ending government monopolies, ensuring greater competition between the public and private sectors, providing a more binding constraint on the budget of losing public sector units and providing incentives to improve performance.

The CPI leader Mr. Inderjit Gupta and many other celebrated MPs said trade unions were not concerned solely with the interests of workers. public sector was a viable instrument of national economy. "you want the BIFR stamp for closure ?" He asked. The Industrial policy statement of July 24,1991 stated that the case of public sector units, which were chronically sick and could not be turned around would be referred to the Board for Industrial Finance and Reconstruction (BIFR) for formulation proposals for their revival. Mr. Inderjit Gupta and Mr. Chandra Shekhar criticised the Finance Minister, Dr. Manmohan Singh, for his statement in Bangkok about the government's proposal to wind up sick units was profit and loss the only yardstick of viability, asked Mr. Gupta. The trade unions were concerned with all factors responsible for losses. A country such as India could not depend on foreign sources in certain sectors and have profit or loss could not be considered the sole factor in deciding the fate of some units. It was a strategic political question, involving the country's sovereignty and independence. The political leaders wondered why Dr. Manmohan Singh was in such a hurry to make a statement on the subject outside the country. The Prime Minister Mr. Narasimha Rao suggested a full-fledged discussion on the functioning of public sector units in the context of the new industrial policy.

Petroleum and petroleum products, electronic items, papers, fertilisers and lots of other items would be imported and now we would have to pay more for them. With the IMF loan, India will be placed further under more debt burdens. India's economy would go out of control. The subsequent abolition of the Cash Compensatory Scheme (CCS) and increase of 1 per cent in bank loans announced by the RBI affected shares in Delhi Stock Exchange immediatly. This had its impact on foreign exchange dealings also. The market was buying more dollars expecting further devaluation in the rupee. Meanwhile, the Reserve Bank of India's curbs on imports were to be lifted in November 1991; Rs. 1,250 crore of Public sector shares offered for sale by the end of December 1991; the government planned to close down unviable public sector units with reference to the Board of Industrial and Financial Reconstruction (BIFR), more foreign banks would be allowed to start operating in India, and inflation was expected to fall to single digit by the end of 1991. The government appeared to be rushing headlong into an exit policy for industry without public debate or an effort at evolving a political consensus. It dealt explicitly with sick public sector undertakings, its thrust suggests that the same orientation would prevail in respect of the private sector too.

Dr. Manmohan Singh made these pronouncements in Bangkok towards the conclusion of the IMF - World Bank meeting on October 16,1991 and declared that the case of some sick public sector companies would be referred to the Board for Industrial and Financial Reconstruction (BIFR) but that the clearly unviable ones would be closed down straight way.

The Federation of Indian Export Organisation (FIEO) President Mr. Ramu Deora said, The suspension of the cash compensatory scheme (CCS) had raised a hue and cry from the exporting community from all over the country. The government could have adopted a more reasonable approach by removing the CCS in phased manner.

"It is an unwarranted step since so many exporters already entered into contracts registering with CCS will incur loss now", reacted Mr. Deora. The REP entitlements as also the enhanced rate for advance licence would give a boost to exports. Exports of tea, coffee, textile, leather, shrimps and handicrafts would get further impetus. But electronics goods exports would adversely be affected.

The ASSOCHAM President, Mr. A. Mazumdar urged the Centre to take "bold economic" initiative to tide over the present balance of payments problem and to overcome the economic crisis. Though the initiatives would be unpopular and harsh, only such steps could help the country to come out of the present mess. The government should come out with long-term fiscal and monetary and export-import policies for a steady and healthy economic growth. Export was not going to increase suddenly. The cost of production would go up, leaving Indian goods less competitive in the foreign market. Factories would be under immence pressure. The impact of the first devaluation of the Indian rupee in 1966 created a lot of problems for the economy then. Many felt the same though they expected it to take sometime to show the impact. Delay in constituting this panel is the main reason behind the government's failure now to dissuade 45 trade unions on November 29, 1991 in protest against the new industrial policy. The government's lackadaisical approach is evident from the fact that it does not have a labour minister just when it is attempting a radical restructuring of the economy.

It is time the government activised the tripartite committee and convinced the trade unions that the human implications of changes being attempted now are being kept in mind. The government must also offer trade unions attractive options to facilitate closure of sick and unviable units. It is a bit puzzling that nearly four months after the announcement for a new industrial policy the centre is yet to define the specifics of an *exit policy*. Little wonder that unware of what *exit policy* means, some trade unions have struck an intransient posture on the industrial policy in particular and economic reforms in general. Once the government lays its cards before the tripartite panel, trade unions may well discover that *exit policy* need not be as inconsiderate as they fear it may be.

Public Sector

The Congress party was opposed to any "indiscriminate" closure of the sick public sector units without taking measure to safeguard the interests of the workers likely to be affected adversely. Highlighting the social costs of structural reforms and technological transformation involved, the government is already working on the line of protecting the labourers who could be adversely affected. It is necessary to involve trade union leaders in formulating and implementing the social component of the reform package. The proposed amendment to the BIFR Act should ensure revival of sick enterprise by putting in managerial and other inputs and in cases where this is not possible, providing a social safety net to protect the interests of the workers.

Dr. Manmohan Singh told the commonwealth finance minister conference at Kuala Lumpur on October 10,1991 that India was not expanding the public sector and did not want this sector to reach commanding heights in the economy. He also spoke on the role of private sector which could play in promoting economic development.

"When we supported public enterprises in the past, we thought they would contribute to capital accumulation and industrialisation, growth and alleviation of poverty", Dr. Manmohan Singh said. But the Public sector served none of these purposes: "we are considering the whole issue afresh. We do not think that the public enterprises should control commanding heights of the exonomy". The government is now considering disposing of 20 per cent of the share of major public enterprises.

The Prime Minister, Mr. P.V. Narsimha Rao told the Lok Sabha on August 26, 1991 that the government would neither jettison public sector, nor stifle indigenous entrepreneurs, but by encouraging capital investment from abroad seek to locate conditions for a quantum jump on the industrial front. Strongly defending the government's new industrial policy, the Prime

Minister said it was neither dictated by some one from outside nor marked any departure from Nehruvian principle. It was the logical development of whatever had been tried in the country on the industrial front in the past, four decades.

The Prime Minister said any more expansion of the public sector which already involved an outlay of Rs. one lakh crore was not possible, given the scarcity of resources in the country. Now the country had to compete with the whole world, there was need for diversification. Even in the industrial resolution of 1956, Pandit Nehru had stated the basic objective of the country was rapid growth. In the circumstances prevailing then, large scale expansion of the public sector was the answer to the country's problems. Now the government felt innovations were needed to achieve the basic objectives of all-round growth of the people: "you should be pragmatic, in tune with what is happening abroad. Instead of conserving jobs, you should think of cost effectiveness involved in more production of goods."

However, a drastic slash in the Centre's investment in Public Sector Enterprises (PSEs) for 1991-92, leaves it 41 per cent lower in real terms than the level five years ago. Budgetary support to PSEs has been placed in the current budget at Rs. 6,829 crores, which is less by Rs. 963 crore even in absolute terms than Rs. 7,792 crore in the revised estimate for 1986-87, according to a study by PTI Corporate Trends. Allowing a 47.4 per cent adjustment for inflation in the period since 1986-87 (including 9 per cent for the current year as projected by the finance minister) this means that the budget estimate for 1991-92 corresponds to Rs. 4,632 crore in 1986-87.

The study says that this year's budgetary support to PSEs is also 10 per cent lower than the revised estimate for 1990-91 of Rs. 7,595 crore. As a result, cut in budgetary support, borrowing through public sector bonds in the current financial year (1991-92) are up by 49 per cent over the budget estimates of the previous year to Rs. 5,869.12 crore. The budget estimate for 1990-91 projected borrowings on bonds at Rs. 3,942.01 crore, which, however, rose by 25 per cent to Rs. 4,932.98 crore in the revised estimate for the same year, according to the budget documents.

Current borrowings through bonds would be higher by 19 per cent than the revised estimates of 1990-91. The figures further reveal that the share of internal resources, bonds, external commercial borrowings and suppliers credit - all of which are classified as Internal and External Budgetary Resource (IEBR) - is upto 77.8 per cent of total investment in PSEs against 72.9 per cent in the revised estimate for 1990-91. The study points out that the actual quantum of borrowings in any year has always been higher than the budgeted figures, essentially because the targets for internal resource generation have never been met.

This pattern is likely to continue for 1991, says the study, taking into account the impact of devaluation on the cost of servicing the external debt of the PSEs and on their import bill. The squeeze on PSEs future earnings will be greater, if the burgeoning burden of interest payments on accumulated borrowings through public sector bond is taken into account, the study adds. An analysis of the public enterprises survey (1989-90) shows that the proportion of both profit and sale that goes towards meeting the burden of loans (including bonds) has risen sharply in the recent years. Interest payment as a proportion of sales, rose five-fold from 1 per cent in 1986-87 to 4.8 per cent in 1989-90, while as a percentage of gross profits they rose from 7 per cent to 29.8 per cent over the same period.

The burden on earnings of PSEs will be further aggravated by the recent measures suggested in the budget for 1991-92 - hikes in interest and corporation tax rates and lowering of depreciation rates. The finance minister's statement, while reviving the interest tax, that financial institutions could reimburse themselves by necessary adjustment in interest rates charged from borrowers, suggested another hike in interest rates, the study pointed out. The slashing of depreciation rates for plant and machinery would mean that profits before tax would go up even without any increase in earnings. Consequently, the PSEs will be paying a larger amount of tax at existing rates, the study notes.

While, this would hold good for firms both in the private and public sector, the changes in depreciation rates would affect the latter more, according to Mr. Waris R. Kidwai, Secretary General of the Standing Conference on Public Enterprises (SCOPE). This is because the public sector is predominant in areas like power, oil and chemicals, which have all enjoyed high rates of depreciation. The study notes that with progressive cuts in budgetary support and increasing dependence on borrowings, the PSEs are being forced into a corner. Hence, they would be forced either to resort to administrative price hike or to cut back on investments, it concludes.

Meanwhile, the annual report of the department of Public enterprises for 1990-91 makes a shocking revelation that 84 enterprises incurred a total net loss of Rs. 2,188 crore during 1989-90, as compared to a net loss of Rs. 1,842 crore during the previous financial year. The report further reveals that the total loss suffered by the top ten loss- making enterprises in the year 1989-90 was Rs. 1,959 crore, topping the list is the fertiliser sector, which incurred a loss of Rs. 356 crore. Poor performance of PSUs is mainly attributable to the subsidies in various sectors such as fertiliser. Statistics showed that the total subsidies amount to a staggering figure of Rs. 80,000 crore, which is 15 per cent of GNP. Other factors for the present economic mess in PSUs are varied, such as financial indiscipline, corruption at many levels of administration, unproductive departments that cause delays, financial excesses indulged in by the States, under disregard for financial or any other sort of public accountability, non-payment of bill by the State Governments etc. The last one, for example, pertains to the state electricity boards, which reportedly have discontinued paying Coal India Ltd and BHEL for supplies of coal and machinery.

In our haste of nation building activity, we have handed over the public sector management to the bureaucracy—

oriented executive wing of the government. Recent studies have shown that over 50 per cent of PSUs have no corporate planning which is the essence of professionalism in the modern management system. Today, we have 242 PSUs with a total capital investment of more than Rs. 100,000 crore and a manpower above 23 lakh regular employees. One could well imagine the magnitude of the losses of these white elephants are enforcing on the national exchequer. If the loss-making PSUs were to be made economically viable, the finance ministry will have to take drastic steps, like giving a free hand to the top professionally qualified management heading these units to stop supplies to all defaulters of payments, so as to instil a sense of financial discipline and management accountability in State Governments, bringing PSUs within the purview of the MRTP Act and launching prosecution against corrupt civil servants. The Central Government should also stop giving debt relief or extra plan allocation on purely political considerations. All these measures should be taken on a war footing before the finance ministry can evolve the proposed clear-cut policy of bringing the erring, loss working units under the axe.

A case study

Two PSUs have faced the axe in Karnataka State. The two companies in question, the Karnataka Implements and Machinery Company (KIMCO) and Mysore Chrome Tanning Company (MCTC), have been chronically ill. "There is no point in pumping the tax payer's money any longer into these sick units", says the State Chief Minister. "In accordance with our declared policy, which has been laid down in the party manifesto, we have decided, in principle, to close down these two companies, because they are non-viable". The share capital of MCTC is just over Rs. 72 lakh, of which over 95 per cent has been invested by the State Government. According to the Chief Minister, the Government has incurred an accumulated loss of Rs. 5.6 crore.

The cabinet sub-committee suggested that the company's assets, like the imported leather processing machinery, the company buildings and the 11 acres of land, could be sold to the private sector and the proceeds of the sale used to compensate its employees as well as to pay off its other liabilities. KIMCO accumulated a loss of Rs. 16.68 crore. It has two units, at Hassan and Bangalore. The cabinet sub-committee recommended the KIMCO be closed down and its employees appropriately compensated. The company had incurred losses of about Rs. 7 crore over the past five years.

Its sales turn over had increased from Rs. 1.68 crore in 1986-87 to Rs. 6.35 crore in 1988-89 fell to Rs. 2.6 crore in 1990-91. This decline was attributed, by the sub-committee, to the Karnataka State Road Transport Corporation (KSRTC) having withdrawn the work orders it had placed with KIMCO. The trade unions refute the contention that surplus manpower is one of the reasons for the decline of KIMCO. They are worried that the Government's withdrawal from the company will affect its labour. The State Government contends that "the interests of the workers will definitly be taken into consideration. At the time of privatisation, the needs of labour welfare will be looked into."

The cabinet sub-committee felt that even with the rehabilitation package, which amounted to about Rs. 11.6 crore, the company would not be able to generate any cash surplus in the next few years. Only the accumulated losses could perhaps be neutralised. The other reason being that financial institutions might have shown greater interest in helping the company if it had a large private sector partner bringing in professional managers to set the company right.

Is the public Sector Relevant ?

The Prime Minister, Mr P.V. Narasimha Rao declared that while Jawaharlal Nehru's policy of having a mixed economy would continue, the government had no funds to expand the public sector any longer. Nor was it possible for the Government to provide budgetary support to sick public sector units. The government's priority now was to arrest sickness in public sector undertakings (PSUs), for there were industries in the public sector which would turn sick if no money was put in them.

The Board of Industrial and Financial Reconstruction (BIFR) would examine the case of each of the sick PSUs. The Government would like to retrieve the position of each of these units. If any impression had gained ground that the sick units would be closed down or that there would be mass retrenchment, it was wrong. For, the government would make all efforts for their recovery. No decision has as yet been taken regarding the future of the chronically sick PSUs. The government, while taking any decision, would ensure that minimum hardship was caused to workers. At the same time, the government did not want the entire country to suffer because of a few sick PSUs. Time had come for government to make the choice of where to put its money.

There were many options before the government for reviving the sick units. Merger of the sick units with the viable ones could be one such option. Modernisation could be another. Each of these cases would be referred to BIFR. of course, BIFR would have to be made more effective and its performance had been commented upon in many quarters. For the first time, PSUs would be referred to BIFR. "What we are going to do, we are not as yet clear" the Prime Minister frankly conceded. Throwing labour out of employment was not the philosophy of the Congress(I) Party. The government was considering ways and means of increasing the National Renewal Fund. Some structural loans had been offered by the international financing agencies, and if necessary, the government would seek more funds. The government would ensure the least hardship was caused to workers.

Before taking a final decision, the government would have talks with Trade Unions of each sick PSUs. The government was also prepared to consider suggestions from any quarter on the issue. The government did not want anyone to get overexcited or worried over the issue. The government was not straying from the Nehruvian model of growth as some people had alleged. The mixed economy would continue and the government had reserved areas for the public sector.

But the fact was that having invested one hundred thousand crore rupees in the Public Sector, the government was not finding it possible to expand it any longer. But that did not mean that the government was dispensing with the public sector. At the same time, the government in future would not resort to nationalisation of any unit. The government burnt its fingers by taking over units left sick by the private sector. And this would not be repeated.

Dr. Pranab Pradhan, Professor of economics at the University of California has offered two major solutions:

First, renovate India's industrial structure on lines of dynamic comparative advantage. This is best achieved by introducing the vital disciplining function of competition and involves movement from the economics of socialism to market socialism.

Second, how can, under market socialism public ownership be combined with the working of the market mechanism ? This can be done by re-organising the public sector enterprises so that public sector managers carry more discretion in entrepreneural decision-making and, at the same time, safeguard against managerial slack.

These two major recommendations were made by Dr. Pradhan delivering the sixth Exim Bank commenement day annual lecture in Bombay on March 17, 1991 on the "State and dynamic comparative advantage", Dr. Pradhan, exploring the role of the State in transforming production and trade, observed that the current world wide movement towards the dismantling of State structure and privatisation emanates from a declining faith in the State and a fundamental belief in bureaucratic incapacity. Yet South Korea and Taiwan are prime examples of aggressive and judicious selective state intervention. The important question is not the extent but the quality of such intervention. He emphasised three aspects of quality of state intervention in East Asia which could be instructive for India.

First, intervention scheme can work closely with the market, and the state has to be alert in using the signals emanating from world markets to judge dynamic efficiency to keep firms on their toes.

Second, state intervention can be selectively targeted to ensure speed and flexibility in the correction of policy errors and re-negotiation of policy goals.

Third, the state can play a role as a pioneer and promoter of industrial transformation in close collaboration and partnership with the private sector.

Critical of indiscriminate and blanket controls and regulations in India, Dr. Pradhan recognised India's slow shift, in times, in the state role as a primary provider of infrastructure and an enabling environment for private as well as public investment to flourish. Emphasizing that competition increases the public visibility of the comparative performance of different public firms. Dr. Pradhan advocated the importance of keeping the doors of international competition open, advocated a fixed duration for infant industry protection and the use of international market signals.

Market socialism combines public ownership with the working of the market mechanism, using the criteria of market competition and market profitability to assess the performance of the public sector. It is particularly important to explore if competitive market socialism can be made economically viable, capable of handling the complex issue of risk taking and innovations, where state socialism has failed.

The experience of the last four decades of planning reveals the complementary role played by the public sector dispite its inefficiencies. In essential, consumption has been encouraged through under pricing of public utilities and other intermediate goods and services produced by the public sector enterprises. To this extent, part of the losses shown by the public sector represent gains for the private sector and the consumers at large. Nevertheless, the question of efficiency of public enterprises remains. By and large, the consensus of opinion has been that it should be possible to improve the efficiency in the working of public enterprises by giving them greater autonomy in decision-making regarding investment, product mix, import mix, pricing and labour management, etc, and by making them accountable to Parliament. These recommendations have not been followed up mainly for lack of political will and bureaucratic indifference. The single biggest source for satisfying the needs of the Indian politician is the public sector, where Rs. 110,000 crore of national wealth is tied up. The return from this investment is less than one per cent per annum, if you exclude the petroleum sector. The blame for this sorry state of affair can be placed squarely on the gross interference by the politician and their flagarant misuse of the resources and facilities of the public sector.

Bureaucracy is held responsible for either being indifferent to the proper implementation of development programmes or for distorting them to the extent where they take a shape never even contemplated by the policy-makers. This has naturally resulted in a growing belief that the path to reform lies in dismantling much of the bureaucratic structure, reducing its areas of jurisdiction and taking more and more activities outside the realm of government intervention. The current wave of liberlisation and its concommittant thrust on the reduction of government intervention has direct relevance principally to the growth of industrial and commercial activities. In these spheres, regulation by bureaucratic institution has, over the years, admittedly served to shackle entrepreneural effort. The curtailment of this power will undoubtedly give a major fillip to the industrialisation of the country.

The institution of the bureaucracy from political interference has been talked about often enough as the first step towards restoring health to the institution. Certainly, no real improvement is possible unless this is achieved and internal control and discipline restored to the system. But the cleaning of the aegaen stables of rules, regulations and exceptions is an equally important measure of reform. What is now required, according to a retired IAS officer, is a powerfully-backed commission with a limited mandate - to simplify procedures, reduce the scope for discretionary decisions at the lower levels and demystify government. Unless this step is taken and taken very soon, we will find that while the forces of industrialisation and commercial activity have been liberated from the trammels of regulation, failure of development programmes in other sectors of the economy will drag down the entire pace of social and economic progress in the country.

Bureaucrats too have their reasons for not favouring privatisation. For career advancement, they must toe the line of the politicians. Many have an itchy palm (the previous cabinet secretary had made a list of nearly 100 IAS officers whose integrity was strongly suspect). Those nearing retirement would welcome a post retirement secure job in the public sector for which the politician's help is needed. Lastly, the bureaucrat is more adept than politician in getting the most out of the public sector. At the same time it is very difficult to induct professionals with the requisite skills in the public sector. Besides, they are not be paid any incentives at par with the private sector.

Privatisation no Cure

Current efforts to privatise the public sector are motivated and unlikely to show the desired improvement in the country's industrial performance, a study by a management expert from the Administrative Staff College of India (ASCI). has said. Various financial indicators and the past record of strikes and lock-outs show that the public sector has performed better than the private sector, says the study by Dr. M.R.K. Reddy, Professor in strategic management at ASCI. The experience and profile of the private sector does not induce sufficient confidence that it can manage complex public enterprises, Prof. Reddy points out giving his findings in a working paper, "the employee side of the privatisation debate."

Inefficiency in public enterprises is primarily due to the failure of the bureaucracy and the politicians. Bureaucratic delays in 300 projects have resulted in an estimated loss of Rs. 75,000 crore and a cumulative delay of over 500 years. It is estimated that the net loss of Rs. 1,719 crore incurred by 102 public enterprises in 1987, could have been wiped out by an increase of just five per cent in capacity utilisation.

Aspects like indiscipline, absenteeism and general lack of work ethos are largely contributions of poor enforcement of legislative and irresponsive and populist attitudes of people rather the pattern of ownership. Given a picture of the state of industrial relations in the two sectors, the study says the past record of industrial conflict in the private sector is no better than the public sector. Though the total employment in the latter is twice that of the former, the number of work stoppage in 1987 were just 396 against 1,121 in the private sector. Against three million lost man days in the public sector in 1987, the private sector recorded 24 million lost man-days.

The human resource quality is also higher in the public sector due to its higher entry level norms in respect of education, skills and training. The privatisation move would thus merely be tactical and time-serving, resulting in overall loss to the economy. Nevertheless, if the government persists with the idea of privatising the public sector, then it would have to strengthen existing social and market mechanisms to ensure responsible conduct by the private sector.

Otherwise, such privatisation may eventually enlarge the list of sick company requiring indirect governmental props, nullifying the original objectives. An analysis would reveal that structural reasons such as market share, product line, growth in industry, etc., at a particular point of time, influence of the indicators of industrial sectors.

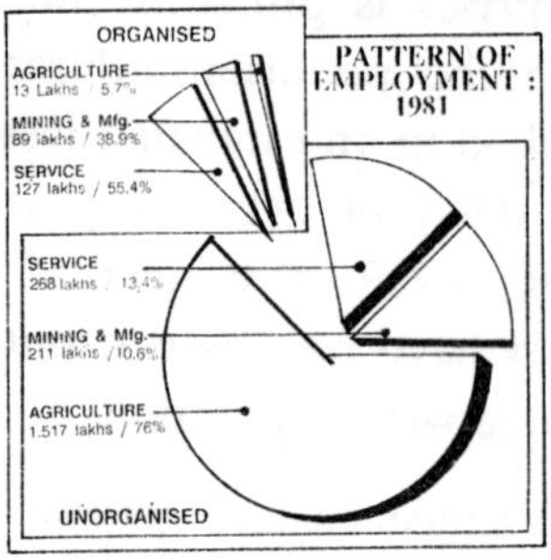

Source: The Sunday Times of India, July 21,1991.

The reported decision of the government to offload by March, 1992 Rs. 2,500 crore of public sector equity on the mutual funds and financial institutions in the first phase has raised fear of a dilution in the quality of the mutual funds' portfolios. Most of the nationalised banks are sick because of their obligation to fulfil the political agenda of successive governments in the past two decades, the mutual funds could also become sick within a few years if we insist on dumping useless bits of paper on them to enable the government to adjust its books.

There is also the fear that large chunks of mutual funds' resources locked up over a period of time, would sharply bring down the market as it is the same funds which are currently supposed to be propping them up. To this Mr. M.S. Verma, Executive Director of SBI Capital Markets, categorically replies that Rs. 2,500 crore will indeed be going out of the market but by March 1992 Rs. 2000 crore of fresh funds are likely to be collected by the funds and the insitutions. The PSU investment will acount for about 5 to 7 per cent of the investible fund of these institutions and that is digestable.

Nevertheless, the public sector did not come to the scene by an accident. There was a convincing case for it, which is best summarised in the Industrial Policy Resolution Act of 1956. The adoption of a socialist pattern of society as the national objective as well as the need for planned and rapid development required that all industries of basic and strategic importance, or in the nature of public capacity services, should be in the public sector. Therefore, the state had to assure that responsibility for the future development of industries over a wider area.

The Public Sector accounts for just eight per cent of the gross domestic savings, whereas it takes a lion's share of 46 per cent in gross capital formation. This means a major part of the investment in the PSUs is financed by private savings, mostly from the household sector.

The Narasimham committee on the financial sector is reported to have indicated that only five public sector banks of the 21 nationalised banks are viable. And worse, the government no longer has the ability to generate the huge funds needed to recapitalise the Public sector banks. The net result of their indiffernt management and the political interference has been that most banks today are highly dust-ridden, making the financial structure of the country precarious. The government has already started negotiating with the World Bank for a US $ 600 million loan to restructure the financial sector. Without this and other loans from international lending institutions, no major restructuring will be possible.

The various proposals under consideration - the selling of loss-making units, selling the equity of profit making units, making the banking sector stronger and more viable - are the first steps towards redefining the role of the PSUs in the country's economic affairs. Consider the so-called exit policy for sick industries. In fact, the new policy aims not at exit but at redeployment. It aims to transfer men, machines and land from low productivity units that have gone bust to high productivity one that will flourish, and in due course enable the payment of higher wage even while providing the consumer with better goods and services. The underlying principle of efficient re-deployment remains.

Nationwide Strike

After a gap of three years, the trade unions organised a nationwide industrial strike on November 29,1991. There were two significant aspects that must be mentioned. One was that after a period of time the trade unions took up issue relating to the country and the common people as a whole and did not confine to trade unions or worker-oriented problems.

The second thing was the overwhelming unit that the trade unions and the Federations were able to achieve this strike would probably go down in history as an agitation in which the maximum number of labour organisations took part.

These were issues like exit policy, delicensing, dilution or near abolition of the Monopolies and Restrictive Trade Practices Act, and the threat to close down public sector units. These issues did not relate to the labour front in isolation. Exit policy gives authority to any industrialist to close the unit without governmental permission. This is done when there are already provisions in the Industrial Disputes Act which permit the industrialists to recommend closure of the unit. The proposed policy militates against the right to wrok. Delicensing and dilution of the MRTP Act would result in conentration of economic power in private hands. Closure of Public sector units would result in large-scale unemployment. The impact of exit policy would be no different.

The Minister of State for Labour agreed that workers have some genuine apprehensions about the new industrial policy announced by the Congress Government. Realising this the Centre had appointed a tripartite committee to go into the entire issue. A full-fledged decision on privatisation of certain sick Public sector units will be taken up in Parliament soon. Nothing would be done without the consent of political parties and trade union leaders. The government did not want to shut down the public sector but only make them more efficient and commercially viable. Out of a total number of 244 public sector units, 135 were giving reasonable returns while 98 PSUs were not doing well. Around 30 to 50 units from the category were chronically sick. The situation was not critical in the sense that the government had over 85 per cent investment on the units that were functioning well while just 15 per cent capital investment were tied up to units which were not up to the mark. In the long run the 20 per cent disinvestment plan of PSUs would benefit the workers. There would be more fund available for investment in new areas which would create additional employment.

A Case Study in Maharashtra State[1]

The trade union leaders observed that the new course of the economic policies, which began in the mid-1980s, has led to the closure of 16,000 to 17,000 factories in the state, that in many cases the affected workers have been denied even their legal dues, that there has been a growing trend of major industrial units in Maharashtra fanning out part of their production operations in the process sizeable proportions of the surplus workers—to units in industrial estates that can produce at a lower cost, an "achievement" made possible by their disregard for statutory obligations, and that entrepreneurs having units in the Bombay-Pune belt seem inclined to celebrate the advent of delicensing by opening new units with labour-saving technologies elsewhere and closing the old ones.

Vivek Monteiro, General Secretary of the CITU- affiliated Mombai Sharamik Sangh, cites the case of Senate (India). This company with a "healthy balance sheet" declared a well lock-out at its Bombay unit about two years ago and installed production facilities at Ankleswar (Gujarat). When its employees secured an injunction against the lockout, the company promptly responded by giving notice of closure of the Bombay unit. The labour leaders are convinced that such trends will get accentuated when the policies initiated by the Narasimha Rao Government take effect.

In fact, the accentuation may have already begun, Monteiro notes that some 8,000 dock workers of Bombay have not

1. *Frontline*, December 6, 1991.

received their wages for three months because of an ill-planned shifting of their work to a new terminal at Nhava Sheva, on the mainland, and the lack of stand-by funds with the Dock Labour Board following the curtailment of subsidies. Monteiro and Datta Samant believe the new policy regime has emboldened employers to resort to questionable pressure tactics in their dealings with labour. The latter says the wrokers of Garlick Engineering have not received their wages for three months and those employed at the race course are being asked to dissociate themselves from his union or face dismissal.

Finance Minister Dr Manmohan Singh's Bangkok statement on the closure of loss making public enterprises has induced widespread concern over the fate of Richardson and Cruddas, an engineering concern with two units in Bombay, and the National Textile Corporation (NTC), many of which mills are located in the city. Monteiro says the services of temporary workers of Richardson & Cruddas are being terminated. Samant says the company's Mulund unit, which has "tremendous capacity" for railway wagon production materials while large orders for wagons go to private enterprises.

In this context of possible closure of the NTC, it is noted that more than one lakh jobs have already been lost in the textile industry in Maharashtra and that the fate of another 25,000 to 30,000 jobs hangs in the balance. Labour leaders in Maharashtra say the "exit policy" which is in the making is the culmination of the establishment's efforts to emasculate the trade union movement in the country.

The strike by industrial workers and government employees on November 29,1991 has highlighted one of the problems that beset the new economic policies. Significant sectors of the economy like the financial services, airline, railways and much of heavy industry were seriously affected. This has pointed to the discontent among a broad spectrum of workers. There is obviously a feeling that a disproportionately large part of the cost of structural adjustment is being demanded from the relatively less privileged in society. The conflicting signals, about the exit policy, privatisation and disinvestment have also contributed to exasperating the sense of insecurity among workers. It is inevitable that like the economy itself, the industrial work force too will have to undergo a degree of restructuring. Employment opportunities are as it is limited, making the scope for redeployment of retrenched labour extremely difficult. Jobs, income and security are, therefore, extremely prized by those who have them. If India has to carry out a successful economic renewal, it cannot afford to antagonise labour efficiency in greater measure than the nature of ownership. International experience shows that privatisation is easily carried out in respect of activities presently profitable or have a hidden potential for success.

If a firm is poor in plant and machinery and is also in an unremunerative product line, there would hardly be any takers for the company except for its real estate value. In conclusion, the study said the pitch for an aggressive privatisation and the attendant new managerialism must be reviewed keeping the apprehensions and questions of the employees in mind. However, there is no contest if the government decides to reduce its participation and activity in future public investments. The government will have to come out with an over all signal of "deregulation", rather than going all-out for privatisation.

Privatisation and Labour Force

Privatisation raises the hackle of trade unionists not only because they fear retrenchment but also because they do not believe the private sector is more efficient. The quintescence of the trade unions has been rudely disturbed by the government's new economic policies and structural adjustments programme which include privatisation programme and spread the fear of widerpread retrenchement. The already large section labelled "unemployed workers" is going to become even larger, unemployment will become a major issue, with jobs becoming even more difficult to get. Massive retrenchment is on the cards too. In fact, statistics corroborate the fact that employment opportunities have been going down both in the public and private sector.

In the private sector it has been more glaring, compared to the 75.25 lakh people employed in 1983, the figure dropped to 73.91 in 1988, marking a drop of 1.61 lakh. in the public sector the figure in 1983 was 164.56 lakh in 1988, it had increased to 183.20 lakh. However, this increase of 18.64 lakh job opportunities is not in proportion to the huge investment made in the public sector.

It should not be forgotten that it was the public sector which increased workers' living standards. The public sector gave the workers' living standards. The public sector gave the worker proper house and basic amenities. What has the private sector done for the workers, except in a few isolated cases like the Tatas ?

Income Per Worker : 1980-81

		Average annual Income per worker (Rs.)	*Annual national income per standardised family of three persons.*
1.	Wages and Salary (A+B)	4,468	4,881
(A)	Organised Sector (1+2)	10,851	4,881
	1. Public	10,643	4,881
	2. Private	11,289	4,881
(B)	Unorganised sector (1+2)	2,482	4,881
	1. Agricultural workers	1,703	4,881
	2. Non-agricultural workers	4,871	4,881
II.	Self-employed (1+2)	3,549	4,881
	1. Cultivators	3,000	4,881
	2. None-cultivators	5,066	4,881
	Total (I+II)	3,948	4,881

Source: The Sunday Times of India. July 21, 1991.

Nearly Rs. 5,000 crore are locked up in hundreds of privately owned closed units. Instead of pursuing privatisation as a policy, attempts should be made to find out who is responsible for the loss in the public sector. It is a gross exaggeration to say that private sector corporations are better managed than the public sector. about 236,000 private sector units are sick. In fact, the public sector makes a much larger contribution to the national exchequer than the private sector. Tax evasion is a habit with the private sector and not with the public sector. Pandit Nehru had called the public sectors "modern temples". and the Congress is today set to tear down these very "temples".

In the meanwhile, as the debate on privatisation and the "exit policy" hots up, a significant phenomenon which had emerged in several parts of the country is one of worker managed industries. Indeed, there are now several instances of workers' co-operative reviving industries rendered "sick" by their original management. A significant aspect of trade union activity in the last few years has been the fact that by and large it has been on the defensive. In West Bengal during 1989 there were only 16 strikes contrasted with 211 lockouts, where as in 1988. there were 34 strikes against 212 lockouts.

The average rate of growth of employment in the private sector in recent years he been less than 0.5 per cent per year, compared to two per cent in the public sector. The workers do not want any privatisation of sick public sector units. What about the 2;36,000 sick units in the private sector ? The workers want an efficient sector, not a public or a private sector. Another apprehension among the workers is that the Finance Minister wants a profit-based, export-oriented economy. This cannot help India in any way.

At present, there are more than 2,00,000 big and small units which are closed, According to a Reserve Bank study, 70 to 80 per cent of the time it has been the owner who have been responsible for the sickness, either because of family quarrels or because of inadequate modernisation to keep pace with the changing time. In Bombay, when Sharad Pawar, Chief Minister of Maharashtra wanted to give milk distributors to private societies, the price of milk shot up by Rs. 1.20 per litre.

This is the end result of privatisation. The consumer will have to pay more.Thus the poor and the workers will be asked to make the sacrifice for the private sector and all the concessions go to the big private business. The privatisation moves will increase sickness and closure, small and medium unit will badly be affected. The import concessions and export obligation will adversely affect public sector units like BHEL, etc. which depend heavily on imports and sell only to the government.

Sick Government Units to Come Under BIFR Purview

The Finance Minister, Dr. Manmohan Singh assured the Lok Sabha on December 4, 1991 that the Bill to amend the Sick Industries Company's Act, was not designed to close the public sector. He tried to allay the opposition fears by emphasising that the government was not anti-public sector, nor anti-workers. The government was as keen as the opposition to ensure that the public sector was saved. The Bill was passed in the Lok Sabha, by a voice vote; despite a walk out by the opposition left parties and Janata Dal members. The bill was amended to enable the Board of Industrial Finance and Reconstruction (BIFR), take up sick units in the public sector. Earlier the BIFR did not apply to the state sector.

This amendment is in keeping with the government intention of running the public sector more efficiently. However, this has also triggered off suspicions in the minds of the working class and the opposition parties that the BIFR would be used to shut- down more and more public sector units. The Finance Minister's reply to the debate was aimed at soothing frayed nerves and attempting to convince the opposition that the government was sincere in its attempts to revive the state owned industrial units. The minister said that sickness in the public sector was not confined to India alone, but a malaise common to developing countries. In China too, a debate was on about the failure of the public sector. Forty per cent of the state owned companies were sick in that country. Dr. Singh felt that the country could not forge ahead if these issues were swept under the carpet. The government was committed to ensuring that the public sector should make a profit. He said that as a well-wisher of the public sector, he could not say that he was happy with its performance.

EMPLOYMENT STRUCTURE 1981

of the organised Seqment of the Indian Economy : March 1989 (in %)

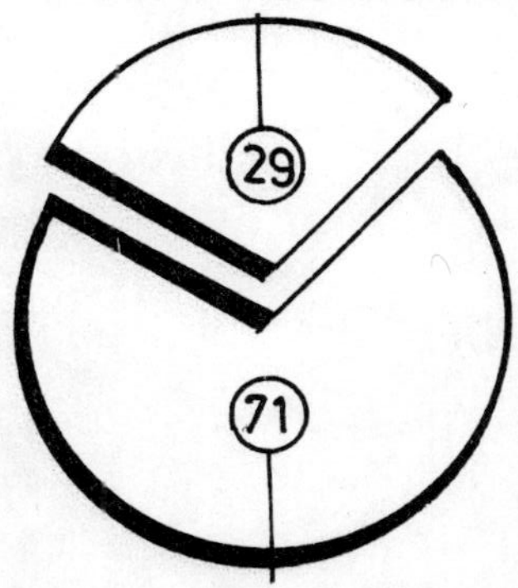

INCOME PER WORKER : 1980-81

	Average annual income per worker (Rs.)	Annual national income per standardised family of three persons
L Wages & Salary (A+B)	***4,468***	***4,4881***
(A) Organised Sector (1+2)	10,851	4,881
1. Public	10,643	4,881
2. Private	11,289	4,881
(B) Unorganised sector (1+2)	2,482	4,881
1. Agricultural workers	1,703	4,881
2. Non-agricultural workers	4,871	4,881
II. Self-employment (1+2)	***3,549***	***4,881***
1. Cultivators	3,000	4,881
2. Non-cultivators	5,066	4,881
Total (I+II)	***3,948***	***4,881***

Source : The Sunday Time of India, July 21, 1991

There was a problem somewhere and the government wanted to correct it. He pointed out that the public sector profits for the year 1989-90, was just 4,48 per cent. If the profit made in the iron and steel sector was taken into account, the percentage would be even more dismal. Hc pointed out in recent years the government had poured around Rs. 1000 crore to provide budget support, but now a limit had been reached. The country could not afford to drain its scarce resources unless a sincere effort was made to improve the working of the public sector. He said that the two options open to the government to continue financing the public sector was by borrowing money either from the domestic market or from international agencies. He explained that no one was willing to pour money into dying concerns.

He appealed to members not to read too much into the bill which was being brought in by the government. Asking the BIRF to help out the sick public sector units was a step in the right direction. He again reminded the House that closure of the public sector was the last option before the government. The Minister told the House that it was not true that the trade unions were not represented in the BIFR. He said that everyone was allowed to appear before the BIFR. and give their suggestions.

By enacting a law the judgement has empowered the Board for Industrial and Financial Reconstruction. This is a shrewd move that casts the responsibility for the closure of patently unviable units on the BIFR and not the government. The BIFR has ordered the winding upto 147 private sector companies to date, but virtually none have acually existed. The reason is that the concerned parties means that nothing further will happen for years. The economy is already paying a heavy penalty for the resources lying frozen in the form of land, machinery and labour in "Moribund Units". Exit policy means not just legal closure but the redeployment of land, machinery and labour in new and productive enterprises, and this cannot be achieved under the present dispensation.

Owners of sick units wants financial institutions to pump in more cash to revive Moribund units, but rarely want to put in any of their own money. The burden ultimately is borne by the tax-payers and bank depositors, whose money goes into this waste. BIFR has demanded power for banks and financial institutions to take physical possession of sick units and liquidate them in cases approved by the BIFR. At present these powers are vested in State Industrial Corporations which have no stake in the recovery of dues or quick redeployment of resources.

Privatisation Plans Finalised

Three optional strategies for privatisation of blue chip public sector companies are now for ready for the government official sanction. Among the companies being considered for privatisation are ONGC, IPCL, Indian Oil Corporation, National Thermal Power Corporation, Air India and Indian Airlines. Shares of these and similarly successful public undertakings will be sold to Indian investment institutions as a first step. Later these shares will enter the capital market. This two-step move is to avoid any possible controversy in case private businessmen succeed in acquiring large holdings.

Strategy one envisages shares worth Rs. 500 crore going to such investment institutions. Optional strategy two looks at a figure of Rs. 2,000 crore. Strategy three is even more ambitious and considers a ball park figure of around Rs. 3,000 crore. However, the employees of the public sector. undertakings protested against the reported move to privatise some of the better managed public sectors. They denied the move which would shift power to the capitalists and hamper development of social uplift. They have seen vested interests in this move. Part of the total shift in government policy was visible in the virtual dismantling of the Public sectors. It is true that in certain Public enterprises and government departments, there is over-staffing, the labour input is in-efficient and there is misuse of trade union power. But, by and large, in the economic system as a whole, labour at work is fully utilised and even exploited, considering the remuneration in relating to the skills and the work put in.

The twin proposals in the new budget (1991-92) to protect workers in Public sector industries from redundancy following closure or restructuring and modernisation, give a strong signal that labour cannot be treated as just another input to be used or discarded according to the dictate of the market. The entrepreneur, in this case, the state, is fully responsible not only to creditors and suppliers, but also to the work force which cannot be made to bear the brunt of the consequence of faulty management. The government has promised a social security mechanism to "fully protect" the interests of workers of public enterprises which are chronically sick and which cannot be turned around, though the details of mechanism have yet to be spelt out.

Public Sector Oil Firms Not to be Privatised

The Union Minister of State for petroleum and natural gas categorically ruled out the privatisation of Public sector oil companies. The government would invest the Oil and Natural Gas Commission (ONGC) with greater autonomy to make it more efficient. Public sector companies like ONGC had an excellent track record and the government's policy was to give "fullest scope" to the public sector to develop: "I can categorically say that the government has no intention to privatise the public sector oil corporations", the Minister said.

It would be recognised to make the ONGC function in a "private sector culture" so that the "commercial decision making was quicker". While revamping the ONGC, the government would ensure that its accountability to government and Parliament was harmonised with commercial decision making. "The ONGC need not come to government for everything". The ONGC's subsidiaries too would be vested with more powers. To a query whether the splitting of ONGC was being contemplated as reportedly suggested by the World Bank, the Minister said there was no such move.

Meanwhile the 5 per cent syndrome may save the country crores of rupees. The latest cost cutting exercise in the public sector is the five per cent. Brainchild of Suresh Kumar, Secretary, Department of Public Enterprises (DPE), there are two aspects to the formula. Firstly, enhance productivity by five per cent. Secondly, reduce costs by five per cent. According to Suresh Kumar, the saving according to the nation from this exercise will be a whooping Rs. 10,000 crore — Rs. 5,000 crore a piece from each operation. Amongst the stringent standards the DPE is likely to implement these are :

(a) **Energy audit:** all PSUs will have to devise energy saving measures. Most units will perhaps be required to conduct an energy audit to apprise themselves of the actual situation and then reduce the load of a minimum of five per cent. There is also some talk that this business of energy audit should be statutory for all units — public as well as private.

(b) **Cost reduction:** all PSUs are required to reduce costs by a minimum of five to ten per cent. While it is unlikely that anyone will be able to cut costs by a drastic ten per cent, a five per cent belt tightening is a pretty feasible exercise.

(c) **Resource generation:** with the planning commission almost committed to non-financing of any PSU requirements and all plans to generate resource from within. This is not an impossibility considering the success of many units like MTNL, Maruti and others to generate a part of their requirements. What the DPE is likely to do is to ask for a minimum 10 to 15 per cent resource mobilisation by the PSUs and make it a part of their Memorandum of Understanding (MOUs).

One of the problems confronting public sector undertakings like Bharat Heavy Electricals Limited (BHEL), Heavy Engineering Corporation (HEC) was poor order booking and plans were evolved to tackle this. The measures contemplated were diversification and vigorous drive abroad to book more orders. The performance of public sector may be highlighted as a whole when PSUs earned a net profit of Rs. 2730.27 crore during 1990-91. It was, however, Rs. 1017 crore less as compared to the previous year. The main reason for this was wages having been increased substantially during the year and this alone led to a decline a net profit by about Rs. 1,000 crore. Added to this was the Gulf crisis and increase in prices of raw materials and other commodities.

It these were taken into account, the net profit of PSUs would have, in fact, been more as compared to 1989-90. The fall in profit of ONGC was substantial (about Rs. 560 crore) and coal, lignite and airline sectors accounted for additional Rs. 365 crore. These together accounted for a drop in net profit of PSUs by about Rs. 925 crore in 1990-91. Poor law and order situation in various states also contributed in its own for the fall in profit through production loss. Militancy has become the order of the day.

Net profit of 181 Central Public Sector Undertakings (PSUs) declined to Rs. 481.28 crore during the first half of 1990-91 from Rs. 1103.25 crore earned by 176 enterprises during the corresponding period of 1989-90. Some of the reasons for decline in profitability were increase in iron and steel price not commensurate with increase in cost for inputs, heavy drop in production due to power failure, etc.

The strike at Bombay Refinery (Hindustan Petroleum Corporation) and flooding of sub-station 132 KVA viz refinery due to cyclonic storm in May, 1990, drop in sales and also charging of operating expenses of Rs. 55 crore from Maharashtra Gas Craker Complex (Indian Petro-chemicals Corporation), which was yet to start production, grounding of A-320 aircraft, adverse change in exchange rate of US dollars and the increased in landing and navigational charge by airport authority (Indian Airline) uncovered gap between price and costs of ships and high interest liability (Cochin Shipyard) etc also contributed to the losses.

If the Finance Minister Dr. Manmohan Singh wants financial discipline, he should prosecute all state corporations that fail to finalise their accounts within six months of the close of a financial year. This may mean prosecuting some of the top civil servants of a State, and perhaps a minister or two. It will mean unprecedently, harsh treatment but surely that is called for in this hour of crisis. Dr. Manmohan Singh wants to slash explicit subsidies, like the one on fertilisers. But a path breaking study (Mundle and Rao) has shown that the bulk of subsidies are implicit and thus hidden from public view. Inclusive of these, total subsidies come to a whopping 15 per cent of GNP, meaning around Rs. 80,000 crore. No less than two-thrids of this is provided by the states.

A study of Tamil Nadu's finance by S. Guhan shows that the State recovers only 12 per cent of the cost of services it provides, meaning that the subsidy is no less than 88 per cent. Nor are subsidies targeted at the poor — 91 per cent of the pump-set subsidy benefits larger farmers.

Another study by Bajaj and Aggarwal shows that things are even worse in Uttar Pradesh. There is little point in slashing subsidies at the Centre but doing nothing about state government and hand-outs. Recently, a news item sounds that the Bihar Government had taken ways and means advance of more than Rs. 500 crore from the RBI, ten times its borrowing limit. Why was the RBI so accommodative ?

For that matter, why did the Centre write off Rs. 966 crore of loans to the states in 1990-91? Why have so many states over the years been given debt relief or extra plan allocation on purely political considerations ? Janos Kornai, the famous Hungarian economist has stressed the importance of a hard budget constraint — of not giving a peny more than budgeted in order to ensure efficiency or accountability. As long as a State Government or public sector manager is confident of getting extra cash for the asking, there is no pressure on them to use their assets productively and efficiently. India has borrowed a huge amount of money, and has to service much of this at around 9 per cent interest in dollar terms (which implies a much higher rate in terms of the depreciating rupee. The private sector may achieve a high enough rate of return but half of all investments is in the public sector, and this fetches diplorably low returns which are negative in the states.

Dr. Manmohan Singh has spoken about the need for economic adjustment, but the greatest adjustment by far is needed from the state governments. Unless the Centre shows more grit and determination, the reforms in New Delhi will be rendered meaningless by the lack of economic reforms in the states. The Prime Minister, Mr. P. V. Narasimha Rao, said on November 10, 1991 that his government's, economic measures and abolition of licences and permits pleased the World Bank, which was now willing to assist India in strengthening its industrial base. These policies also powered the way for increased foreign investment. The restructuring of the economy and industrialisation could not be pursued if such similar measures were not pursued vigorously in the states.

The Union Finance Minister, Dr. Manmohan Singh urged the state governments to urgently order fiscal restructuring of the loss incurring electricity boards, introduce cost-based-tariffs and bring about operational improvement in the power systems if the development aspirations of the people were to be realised. Dr. Singh said that continued financial crisis in the State Electricity Boards could deprive the country over US $ 1 billion funds from external multilateral agencies every year with serious implications on the overall economic development. He said that multilateral agencies were reluctant to commit fresh investment in the power sector because of the institution and financial porblems of the electricity board. The financial crisis in the power sector could be gauged from the fact that 13 out of 17 existing electricity boards were in the red with cumulative losses soaring to Rs. 4,500 crore as on March 31, 1990. As a consequence power cuts were in force in most parts of the country and grid collapses were becoming fairly common.

Informed sources said that the National Thermal Power Corporation (NTPC) and Government of India had taken up the issue with the major defaulting states including Bihar. So much so that the Centre has also decided to adjust the money coming out of coal cess against the oustanding dues with the NTPC. During 1990-91, NTPC received Rs. 255.15 crore through central appropriation. Another Rs. 155.98 crore was received through central appropriation for 1991-92. Decision had been taken by the Centre that all the outstanding dues would be paid to NTPC through central appropriation in a phased manner and over period of four years. The outstanding dues at that time stood at Rs. 1100 crore which had now gone up to Rs. 1449 crore. All efforts were being made to get the letters of credit enhanced from Rs. 99.08 crore to Rs. 126.45 crore. It has also decided to revise the tariff according to the recommendations of the K.P. Rao Committee.

In addition to this, the poor quality of power supply forced consumers to purchase costly back-up generating equipment which used scarce liquid fuel. During 1990-91, only two electricity boards achieved the statutory minimum surplus of three per cent of the value of net fixed assets. The electricity boards' contribution to the Seventh plan from their own resources was minus Rs. 1,812 crore and projections for the Eighth plan indicated that this would increase further to minus Rs. 11,265 crore, thus holding a dismal prospect not only for the State Electricity Boards but also for the power sector. Money is power. That, at least, is the way the government views the development of the energy sector. So, the Narasimha Rao regime is turning to private sector for the funds required to create energy capacity. The states are also relying on private industries to meet their electricity requirements. The energy sector needs Rs. 1,000 crore project. Hundred- crore projects will not do.

The Eighth plan approach paper, cleared by the cabinet in October 1991, expressed fears that any reduction in plan outlay for public sector investment may lead to a situation "of a kind that prevailed in the 1970s. When shortages of cement, steel, coal and power were severe", and "the rate of inflation was 20 per cent".

The approach paper has further stated that any attempt by the government to accept a selective role for the public sector should be looked at from all sides, As the paper explains, "since projects have long gestation period in the infrastructual sectors, the investment in the immediate future determine the long term growth possibilities for the economy." While the paper accepts the fact that private sector investment can reduce the need for investments in the Public sector, it apprehends a "lag" between policy changes and actual investment. Even in his budget speech, the Finance Minister had stated that "the portfolio of public sector investment would be reviewed so as to concentrate the future operations of the public sector in areas that are strategic for the nation, require high technology for the economy, and are essential for the infrastructure.

However, the above views are in direct contrast with the actions initiated by the political leaders. The budget for the year has attempted to keep a check on planned expenditure in the hope that the shortfall will be bridged by the private sector, which can now enter areas higherto reserved for the Public sector. The new industrial policy, following similar logic, has eased the entry to foreign investment and domestic entrepreneurs into new areas. The Finance Minister has also decided to follow the philosophy of financial discipline whereby the various ministries have to keep a check on their expenditures and keep within the budgetary allocations.

However, the plan paper states that a mere liberalisation of policies does not lead to immediate investments by the private sector. The paper cites two examples to illustrate this point.

"The power sector has been opened up for the private sector but the response has not been adequate." The problem issues relating to distribution and bringing of power will, according to the paper, take a few years between being sorted out between the private sector and the State Electricity Boards. "Similar has been the experience of the fertiliser projects assigned to the private sector". Under the given constraints, the

Eighth plan paper has estimated that the outlay on public sector for the plan period (1992-97) can be reduced to Rs. 4,00,000 crore which will be equivalent to 43.2 per cent of the total domestic investment. But the paper wants that such a move "will require more harsher decisions".

The paper, however, points out that such a reduction is not possible as investments on all infrastructural projects cannot be reduced. "Selectivity is the key" to the new approach of reducing the investment outlay of the public sector in the next five years. Thus the conclusion seems to be that the above estimate assured in 1990 by all the ministries for formulating a "sectoral profile of investment in the Public sector may be the right basis for the Eighth plan."

According to this estimate which was subsequently upgraded this year after taking into account the various cost escalations, the Public Sector would invest Rs. 4,21,000 crore in the five year period, of which Rs. 61,000 crore would be for current outlays. This investment is equivalent to 45 per cent of the total domestic investment. The figure of Rs. 4,21,000 crore, in terms of percentage, is similar to the investments on the public sector during the whole of the Seventh Plan and the two previous five year plans. Hence, the role of the Private sector, in terms of investments, may be similar to the last 12 years.

However, the paper has cautioned the government not to report the decisions followed during the two annual plans of 1990-91 and 1991-92. In these two plans, no money was allocated for future projects and only on-going ones received the attention of the finance ministry. Such a policy could lead to "infrastructual bottlenecks" which will mean an era of storages like the 70s.

The Eighth plan had envisaged an incremental capital of 38,369 MW in power sector to meet the energy shortfall. Its implementation would require funds for Rs. 1,20,000 crore approximately. While in 1988, a new project or a fresh grassroot plant would cost Rs. 1.5 crore per MW. today it has doubled to nearly three crores. So, the government's radically changed stance on allowing a private party into the core sector was no big deal. It had no other option. The budget 1991-92 announced the significant withdrawal of the Monopolies and Restrictive Trade Practices (MRTP) Act in the case of the power sector. The post-budget also announced that multi-nationals and foreign companies could own outo 100 per cent of the equity in a power project.

The major hurdle in the way is the Electricity Act (1946) which governs the generation and distribution of electricity. Industrialists object to such positions as the restrictive tariff rates and the fact that a private party is not allowed to distribute the power itself. They have to sell it to the SEBs where private parties already exist, such as the Tatas in Maharashtra, they can only function as the licencees of the SEBs - and the licences are to be renewed at regular intervals. Further, rates of depreciation on plant and equipment are low. Conscious that these provisions may act to inhibit private entry into the power sector, the government has offered few incentives. These include raising the debt equity ratio to 1:4 and increasing the rate of return on capital employed from 12 to 15 per cent. But these have not been enough. And private enterprise seems convinced that whoever rules in New Delhi over the coming years, will have no option but to open up the energy industry, because the government lacks the huge funds to make fresh investments with energy sector.

Chapter VI

World Bank's Warnings to Power Sectors

The World Bank (WB) had taken a very serious view of the worsening arears position and is pressurising the National Thermal Power Corporation (NTPC) and the government of India to take immediate remedial measures or else it might not finance future projects. The World Bank provided an assistance for NTPC aggregating to US $ 382.10 million. During 1990-91 a loan agreement of DM 60 million was entered with KFW of Germany towards local expenses for Dadri Gas project. It has also signed an export credit for French Franc 1,641 million for funding of French goods and services required for the Kawas project. These include gas turbine, gas turbine generators and steam turbines. The new projects likely to be taken up by NTPC also include the North Karnataka thermal power project in Hazaribag district with an installed capacity of 1000 MW. The NTPC has decided to set up pilot cum demonstration plants and participation in joint venture for manufacture of fly ash based projects.

Meanwhile the 600 MW Farakka Super Thermal Power project of the NTPC generated 343 million units of energy at a plant load factor of 77 per cent in October 1991. This is the highest generation achieved by the ever since its inception in 1986. The previous record for generation was 337 million units in March 1991. It also received a record quantity of coal at 303.000 tonnes in October 1991. The first unit of 500 MW capacity is scheduled to be commissioned next year while work on the second unit of same capacity was in progress.

According to the latest Economic Survey of the Government of India, the backlog of outstanding unutilised aid was a staggering Rs. 55,000 crore, as on April 1,1991. Even at the currently depreciated value of the Indian rupee, this works out to approximately US $ 25 billion. In the context of the mounting fiscal deficits and the paucity of foreign exchange resources, the issue of unutilised foreign credit assumes great importance. The road blocks to its speedy utilisation are many, and some of them are rooted in the way large projects have to be managed in the Indian environment. By the end of March 1992, the unused amount count rises to Rs. 60,000 crore—more than the budgeted tax revenue of the Central Government for 1991-92.

The Annual Flow of External Assistance

Year	External Assistance Authorisation	(Rs. in Crores) Utilisation	Utilisation rate (%)
1984-85	4880	2354	48
1985-86	5650	2936	52
1986-87	6160	3605	59
1987-88	9265	5052	55
1988-89	13070	5304	41
1989-90	10826	5802	54
1990-91(p)	6252	6660	107

Source: The Illustrated Weekly of India, October 26-November 1,1991.

One must realise that at any given time a portion of sanctioned credit is bound to remain unutilised. There are three main reasons for the gap between sanction and utilisation—the generation periods in project implementation, the nature of the assistance, and the procedures of the low utilisation. As the composition of this unused amount will reveal below that much of it is earmarked for project which have long gestation periods. A power plant, for example, may take years to complete from the time of conceptive.

End use sectors of unused credit

	As % to total outstanding
Transport & Communication	10.51
Power	36.01
Iron and Steel	2.66
Industial Development	24.94
Agriculture Development	13.18
Oil and Petroleum Products	1.47
Others	11.23

Source : The Illustrated Weekly of India, October 26-Nov. 1, 1991.

The foreign assiatance is mostly to finance the import portion but the local activities and the creation of necessary infrastructures have to be financed locally. Experience shows that projects, invariably, require the active participation of state governments, local bodies, a couple of more central ministeries and the public at large. Even with the falling participation rates, the World Bank and its affiliate, the International Development Association (IDA) are still major funding agencies. Together they constitiute more then 45 per cent of all the sanctioned credit. The IDA assistance is the best, since it carries no interest charge. However, 0.75 per cent is levied as a service charge on the disbursed amount and 0.75 per cent commitment charge is levied on the undisbursed amount.

The World Bank loan is costlier, with varying rates of interest, the current rate being in the region of 7.5 to 8.5 per cent. The World Bank and the IDA have together sanctioned loans aggregating US $ 28.8 billion, of which US $ 2.8 billion were sanctioned during 1989-90. The commitment charge on even 20 per cent of the undisbursed amount at the rate of 0.25 per cent would be close to US $ 15 million—adequate to import about half a million barrels of crude oil, even at the currently inflated price. Agencies like the World Bank have clearly indicated that future project funding will depend on past use, changes in project management and a host of other things.

The main factors for the under-utilisation of assistance are believed to be the time say between commitments and the conclusion of specific credit arrangements, time consuming procedures, governing procurement of stores and equipment, delays in land acquisition for construction work and domestic budgetary constraints in providing counter part fund. Given the present shortage of foreign exchange, high priority has been given to the utilisation of unused external assistance.

Lending country institution	Authorisation Rs in crores	% to total	Utilisation Rs in crores	% to total
	Aid authorisation and utilisation Cumulative totals as on 31st March 1990			
World Bank	21547	24.88	10565	19.52
IDA	15880	18.34	13007	24.03
USSR	14028	16.20	2244	4.15
USA	6615	7.64	6411	11.84
Japan	5470	6.32	3615	6.68
Germany	4206	4.86	3506	6.48
UK	3985	4.60	3699	6.83
Canada	1965	2.27	1325	2.45
France	2235	2.58	1823	3.37
Total	86599	87.68	54129	85.34

Source: The Illustrated Weekly of India, October 26-November 1,1991.

The World Bank is concerned at India's mismanagement of the power sector and its inability to carry out promise and commitments to the bank which has led to suspension of further loans in that area until the government take a remedial action. A country's industrial growth can be directly linked to its power supply prospects. In fact, the power sector has a weightage of 11.4 per cent in the index of industrial production. The lack of this crucial input is putting a serious crimper in the plans of industries, especially in the eastern sector, and the southern sector. The world Bank Vice-President, Mr. Attila Karaosmanglu, said the waste and mismanagement in the power sector, in particular, are costing India dear. The bank has money to lend (some analysists put it at the less than US $ 1.5 billion) but it cannot do so unless it sees economic reforms in place to make the power projects viable.

Asked how he would explain "this mess" when obviously the bank had approved the projects, the procurement was on the basis of global tender, the bank apparently supervised the implementation and followed through, Mr Karaosmanglu gave an answer which he himself described as "blunt". He said: "Procurement in India takes much longer than in other countries in the power sector. We have taken in many instances the guarantee given to us by State Electricity Boards or the people involved in power on their face value. When they said they would make the necessary adjustments in the power rates, they would make the necessary connections, reduce losses, etc, we took them in good faith. They did not prove to be deliverable on the part of the people who promised us".[1]

Asked whether it was time that half a billion dollars which India could have had for the power sector from the bank was being witheld, Mr Karesmonoglu said:

"At this point, I cannot tell you whether the numbers are correct".

"You may be referring to numbers related to possible new projects, some of which have already been prepared but which we cannot present to our banks. Some may be expected to be completed. But there is a huge amount of resources involved which, unfortunately, we do not feel yet can be given a go-ahead in the power sector in a revitalised and energised way".

Mr Karaosmonoglu recalled the heavy involvement of the World Bank in the power sector in India over many years. The implementation of projects in that sector turned out to be slower than "we all hoped to see". The financial viability of the power entitles "has not been to levels which would give confidence that the power sector could be increasingly more self-financing, self-sustaining and viable in its future developments".

India, Mr Karaosmonoglu said, needed very heavy investments in power. Future growth would put quite a bit of additional demand. However, "We feel unless the financial viability of the institutions is achieved, it would be a wasteful

1. The Times of India, New Delhi, September 13, 1991.

effort on our part to continue making new loans or even disbursing an existing loans in certain cases".

The Indian power sector, he said, was institutionally quite complex. In terms of financing institutions for power transmission for power, origins of power such as thermal, hydro, etc, and in terms of actual management of generation and distribution, there were federal as well as state institutions.

The performances of some state electricity boards were particularly weak, their rates were low and their losses were large. Their efficiency as a result was in, need of quite a bit of improvement. The World Bank had been discussing these problems of general adjustments and improvements with different state governments in India for the last three or four years more intensively.

Meanwhile, the government is making concerted efforts to bridge the demand-supply gap in power, which is expected to rise sharply in future due to anticipated accelerated economic growth. The government planned to optimise nation's available resources and was likely to spend about Rs. 1,200 crore on the renovation and modernisation of old power stations. Since the fiscal resources would be a major constraint, it was necessary to use that technology which would help increase power generation. Many old plants set up in 1960 and 1970 were operating at low load factors of 25 to 40 per cent but were capable of substantial improvement through re-powering. They already possessed the infrastructures and could be re-powered in three years compared to 4 to 6 years for a new power plant.

Meanwhile, the World Bank has been warning the government to make reforms in power sector. It has also been pressing the energy ministry to help the National Thermal Power Corporation (NTPC) to get its monies back from the loss-making state electricity boards (SEBs). But to no avail. Eventually the World Bank has taken matters into its own hands.

Point of no Return

The authority was negotiating for two loans:

1. US $ 375 million for NTPC thermal power project, and (2) another US $ 250 million for the Power Finance Corporation (PFC). The World Bank has frozen both. Other things are also threatened, according to a news report.[2]

1. Assistance to three SEBs — those of Karnataka (US$ 262 million), Kerala (US $ 198 million) and Himachal Pradesh — would be severed by September 30,1991, if certain stipulations of the bank are not fulfilled.

2. The Karnataka SEB would lose out on bank loans if there is no improvement in returns. The projected figure for the fiscal year 1991-92, is US $ 4.93 This is unacceptable. Not long ago, the Uttar Pradesh SEB had felt the axe. The World Bank suspended its US $ 350 million assistance because it could not push its rate of return to three per cent in the fiscal year 1990-91.

"This is clearly an alarming situation", said an official of the Department of Power in the Minsitry of Energy. Added Karosmanoglu, in Washington:

"The Bank has reached the point where it would like to pause and wait for productive action by India before going ahead with the projects". This is not going to be easy.

SEBs remain the biggest stumbling block — 13 SEBs are in the red. Their total losses stood at Rs. 4,500 crore at the end of March, 1990. They did not contribute to the internal re sources but actually drew from the Seventh Plan: to the extent of Rs. 1,812 crore.

For the Eighth plan, their demands are staggering: Rs. 1,20,000 crore to add 39,000 MW of generating capacity.

---

2. *Sunday* 29 September-5 October, 1991.

None of this is hidden. State Power ministers met three times in less than a year. Both the union finance minister and the energy minister have pleaded for improvement in the SEBs' performance. Deficiencies arise because of the project delays, resulting in timc loss and lost overruns, inadequate budgetary support, constraints regarding acquiring land, environmental clearances and rehabilitation plans, constitute infinite drains on the SEBs. At the same time, there is no comprehensive plan to address these vital matters.

Subsidised electircity to the agricultural sector, bled the SEBs almost limitlessly. The state governments overstretch themselves to provide electricity at a sixth of the actual cost of generation (16 paise per unit versus a production cost of 92 paise) without a cost-plus formula of pricing, the system is unsustainable. The state government repeatedly assure the SEBs of covering up the expenses incurred because of the power subsidies to the farm sector and renege on their promise just as regularly.

While following such a debiliting price-policy, the states are threatening the viability of the central power plants too. The NTPC, NHPC, NEEPC and DVC which feed the various national grids, have huge outstanding bills from the state governments. NTPC is owed Rs. 1648.83 crore, NHPC Rs. 171.19 crore, NEEPC Rs. 91.34 crore and DVC Rs. 399.56 crore.

"The bank's stipulations that apply to the SEBs apply to us too", said an NTPC official. "Therefore, the World Bank's financial assistance to us is also threatened". The situation is not likely to improve until the SEBs are whipped to shape. And because of a constitutional conundrum, the centre is helpless. SEBs lie within the administrive control of the state governments. But at the time, the Central government guarantees loans to SEBs from the global bilateral and multinational agencies. As a result it takes the rap too.

Consider the case of the gas-based power plants run by the NTPC. By their very nature, gas based plants generate power at more cost than thermal or hydel ones. But the HBJ pipelines are executed at huge costs and the gas it carries have to be utilised. Hence NTPC's gas-run turbine electricity costs Rs. 1.75 a unit. The matching price for local power: between 92 paise to Rs. 1.12. No state government wishes to draw electricity from these guzzlers. And when power deficit states like Uttar Pradesh are compelled to, they decline to honour the higher costs. Results: a no-win situation. NTPC and the centre have tried to score several times. And failed. NTPC has threatened to shut down its plants. The centre on its part has vowed to suspend assistance to the state. Against outstanding of Rs. 2310.92 crore, only Rs. 325 crore were recovered from the states by the central government. The peaceful way is to meter the supplies to agriculture. If the power managers do not tone up their business, they could neutralise the benefits of liberalisation that economy awaits.

Central Takeover of Power

The Union Minister of State for power and non-conventional source of energy has offered central takeover of power generating units in Bihar if the state government failed to improve the power situation. The Bihar government failed to improve the deteriorating power situation in the state. Owing to lack of power maintenance, all generating units had been producing owefully low quality of power. If the state government is not capable to run the generating units properly then it should hand over all the units to the centre. The centre will bring all units back on rails".

Only 26 per cent plant load factor in the existing power generating unit in Bihar was lowest in the country. All generating units in Bihar had capacity to produce 1200 MW in the state. But only 200 MW was being generated per day in these units. The centre had recently approved an ambitious hydro-electricity Koel-Karo project for the state. The project will be completed in the next seven years. Owing to procedural wrangles, the project was hanging fire for the last 13 years.

Apart from this, the state would get another breakthrough in power sector. The work on 400 KVa transmission line from

Bihar Sharif to Varanasi would be completed soon, resulting in abundance flow of power to state from Singrauli Power project. The first Unit of 210 MW power project in Kahalgaon was commissioned on November 19,1991, on the occasion of birthday of late Mrs. Indira Gandhi. The Electricity Act had been suitable amended to facilitate private sectors for generating power in private sector. The centre and different state governments received offers of generating 25,000 MW from private sectors so far with the amendment in the Act. A private company, meanwhile, offered to generate 400 MW of power in Chandil in Bihar. The Bihar government was yet to send any proposal in this connection.

The central government blamed both the Bihar and West Bengal governments for making a mess of the affairs of Damodar Valley Corporation (DVC). The DVC had been facing crisis due to apathetic attitude of these governments. The Bihar government alone owes a sum of Rs. 400 crore of the DVC.

The Indian industrialists laid the blame squarely on politicians, while the politicians felt that the work culture of public sector managers was responsible for the lamentable state of affairs. Both were indulging in some plain speaking. Brave words could be exchanged. But this clearly highlighted the yawning gap in performance between the public and private sectors. It focussed on the power sector with special reference to the incredible loss-making machine otherwise known as the State Electricity Boards (SEBs). It projected the benefit which could accrue from privatisation. In 1989-90 private sector generators earned a net profit of 7 paise per unit of power while SEBs lost Rs. 3,759 crore while private corporations made a profit of Rs. 116 crore. In the current year 1991-92 losses are estimated to exceed Rs. 4,500 crore.

In just four years from 1987-88 to 1990-91, the SEBs have chalked up losses to the tune of Rs. 14,000 crore—enough to credit almost 10,000 MW of additional capacity. Worse, their performance is deteriorating year after year. Significantly, if the SEBs had miraculously improved capacity utilisation from 53 per cent to 70 per cent as in the case of the private sector, they would have generated an additional 3,000 MW of power in 1989, but at the same time would have lost another Rs. 1,400 crore. An expert asked this question—how do the SEBs manage to lose such prodigious sums while the private companies earn a return of more than 4 per cent on capital employed with the same rates for raw materials paid by both? Of course, answers are obvious: inefficiency and mismanagement in the public sector undertakings.

What makes power generation attractive to private sectors like the RP Goenka group, Century Spinning Mills, a Birla Group and the Tatas which have had already a base in the power sector? It is the kind of sops that are being offered. Be sides allowing even multinationls 100 per cent equity participation, all private companies entering the power sector will be allowed a debt-equity ratio of 4:1.

Debt-Equity

The Government has ruled out any change in the 4:1 debt equity ratio, it has already announced to encourage private investments in the power sector. Private corporations have been demanding that the debt equity ratio should be increased to 6:1 because of the huge outlay required for power generation. In an effort to overcome the chronic power shortage in the country, the ministry had decided to throw open the sector for private participation. The results have so far been far from encouraging. Yet the government is unwilling to be pressurised by the private sector. Ministry sources maintain that the debt equity ratio had been fixed after taking into account the views of the private sector. It was not a rate arbitrarily determined by the government. As such the government is in no mood to give in to the lobby for an increase in the equity ratio.

The Public sector will be permitted to raise up to 20 per cent of their outlay form the public. In order to safeguard the return of investment against possible under-demand of power, arising from variations in demand patterns the government is permitting the generating companies to sell power on the basis of structured two-part tariff. This will be based on the operational norms and the optional plant load factor (PLF) prescribed by the government from time to time. According to the Centre for Monitoring the Indian Economy (CMIE), power generating during 1990-91 fell short of the requirements by about 7.9 per cent. The government sources also indicate that the country's requirement of an additional 38,000 mega watts (MW) of power during the Eighth Plan period was, in fact, sealed down to 28,000 MW, leaving a huge gap.

During April-December 1990, the electricity generated was 194 billion units as against a target of 200.6 billion units. Experts claim that in the present circumstance, judging on the basis of power generation during the first nine months of the current year 1991-92 the annual growth rate will not go above eight per cent.

Nevertheless, the ministry of energy is also firm in keeping the rate of return at 5 per cent above the rate of credit fixed by the Reserve Bank of India. Senior officials feel that the private sector has no reason to grumble, as the government is ensuring that it is protected from loss. Risk has to be taken in every business venture, and the power sector is no exception. The government exchequer is evidently in no position to subsidise the grossly inefficient SEBs or invest much needed fund to give electricity production a boost. In the Seventh Plan, the SEBs were estimated to have collectively lost Rs. 11,300 crore. A whopping 63 per cent of this was said to have been on account of the concessional tariffs given to various sectors. The major culprits are the concessional tariffs for agriculture and transmission and distribution losses. In a statistical analysis, the paper reveals that if the agricultural concessions had not been in place, SEB losses in 1989-90 would have fallen from Rs. 3,759 crore to Rs. 405 crore. And the accumulated losses from 1987-88 to 1990-91 would have plummeted from Rs. 14,000 crore to less than Rs. 500 crore. On an average SEBs charge 15 paise per unit from agricultural use - a clear subsidisation of the rural rich since the landless and the marginal farmers seldon use power extensively. Industrial users, on the other hand, are charged an average of Rs. 1.05 per unit. In

1989, the SEBs lost Rs. 2,165 crore, thans to the subsidised power granted to the rich farmers. With state governments in no position to subsidise the SEBs, they were left with no choice but to bear the unnecessary economic burden.

Private companies reported an average transmission loss of 14 per cent in the period 1987-90 while the SEBs managed to lose 20 per cent. The Delhi Electricity Supply Undertaking (DESU) initially, reported a staggering transmission loss of 26 per cent. Similarly, fuel consumption in SEB's was 12.2 ml per unit compared to 5 ml per unit for the private generation companies. What improvements could privatisation bring forth if one assumes that the SEBs will eventually perform at par with the private companies? The inadequate and erratic supply of power was also quite obviously, one of the factors that contributed to make India an unattractive option for the multinationals, despite the other clear advantage. The CMIE estimates that by 1994-95, the country will face a deficit of about 2,908 million unit of energy.

For starters, power generation will improve with capacity utilisation going up to 70 per cent. In 1990-91, that would have meant an additional 3,500 MW of power. This would have practically wiped out of the 7 per cent gap between demand and availability.

In conjunction with an increase in tariffs for agricultural use from 15 paise per unit to 43 paise per unit, the SEBs would have generated an additional revenues of Rs. 5,000 crore. With private sector parameters of input use in place (for instance 5ml of fuel per unit against 12 ml per unit prevailing now), the increase in costs due to additional generation has been calculated at Rs. 1000 crore. That leaves surplus of Rs. 4000 crore with the SEBs — enough to wipe out losses to be incurred in 1990—91.

The power sector, from a purely financial point of view, should be attractive enough for both the Indian private sector and the multinationals. The Bombay Suburban Electric Supply Ltd (BSES) in 1990-91, had a 23.09 per cent return of net worth, while the return on funds employed was 21.37 per cent. The Ahmedabad Electric company, though not quite as impressive, too had a 6.20 return on net worth and a 2.35 per cent return on funds emloyed. The Tata Power Company, a part of the Tata Electric Companies Troika, had a return on net worth that amounted to 10.74 per cent, while their return on funds employed come to 4.22 per cent.

While the government has been loudly proclaiming its intention to invite foreign participation, it has not gone down to basics. For instances, so far the mechanism for repatriation of profit for overseas investors has not been announced. Though officials in power ministry say that the planning commission has agrued in principle to allow foreign firms to take their profit out of the country, no official announcement has been made. Private participation in the power sector will have to be put off until a special task force in the power ministry submits its findings on a comprehensive two-part tariff structure. The two-part tariff structure divides what has to be paid to a generating company into two parts — a fixed charge and a variable charge. The fixed charges, by and large, cover sunken costs and do not vary with the level of generation at a station, whereas variable changes represent additional costs related to actual generation.

Indian companies too, except those like the Tatas and the Goenkas, who are already in the power sector, have been hesitatant to take the plunge, considering their doubts about the quality of investment required. The ministry is not helping matters by taking a rigid stand. Ministry sources are quick to point out that atleast three projects where private companies are allowed has been sanctioned and work started.

However, despite the attractiveness of the power sector on the books, the most crucial component that will determine the success or failure of the government move will be the pricing of electricity according expert opinion. The new private sector companies in the field are being allowed the choice to operate as a generating company to sell bulk power to the grid, much like Tata Electric does in Maharashtra or to operate as a license and generate its own power and sell it to consumers through its own supply and distribution lines. The government has stated that once the sale rate is fixed, no limit will be imposed on the actual profits generated by the companies. However, the past record of the government does not give much encouragement. In the past, the various power subsidies offered to various sectors of the economy, especially agriculture, have largely been responsible for the poor performances of the various SEBs.

Bilateral Aid : Freeze to Continue

According to newspaper sources the existing freeze on the use of bilateral aid for new power projects will continue till maching rupee resources are found to utilise the undisbursed bilateral aid already in the pipeline. This was decided at a high-level review meeting convened by the finance ministry in the beginning of November 1991 following insistence by the Ministry of Energy that India must seek fresh bilateral aid for power projects during the Eighth plan period. The review meeting decided that before any dicision was taken on the issue, an assessment should be made of the total investment needed in power sector during the Eighth plan period and the availability of rupee resources for ongoing projects.

The current undisbursed bilateral aid, according to the latest figure with the finance ministry, is placed at Rs. 21,000 crore. In 1990-91, India used bilateral aid for the power sector only to the tune of Rs. 1119 crore as against the traget of Rs. 3,500 crore. The government decided against going for fresh power projects financed by bilateral aid in January 1990. It was found that such projects were at least 40 per cent costlier than projects funded by multilateral agencies like the World Bank as there is no global tendering. Because of the delay in execution, the cost of the projects also goes up due to the depreciating rupee, thus injecting a built-in inviability in the project.

A case in point is the Aanpara project being set up with Japanese assistance. The project has been stalled mid-way because the U.P. government has no funds to complete it; while the Japanese Consortium has already supplied a major part of the required plant and equipment. It is now estimated that the cost of power generated by Aanpara would be around Rs. 3 per unit. A situation has thus been brought about in which the very generation of power in this station would only add to the losses of the state electricity board since power tariff in the state is just about half this cost if not lower.

The irony is that the country is self-reliant in power technology. The government owned Bharat Heavy Electrical (BHEL) has stabilised its 200 and 500 MW units, but the government does not have the adequate funds to plan new projects in the sector. Most of the state electricity boards are also bankrupt so that there is no question of their generating internal resources for investment in new projects. Official sources say that there is little possibility of the private sector's participation in the power sector in a big way until the issue of power tariff and distribution is resolved. The minimum cost of generation assuming that the private sector is able to set up a plant in record time, would be Rs. 2.05 paise per unit. The state electricity board will have to pay this minimum price for buying power from the private sector. it will be able to do so only if the tariff is substantially hiked.

The government, however, will not stand in the way of the private sector availing of suppliers' credit to finance power project. Thus the Rs. 1200 crore Budge-Budge power project in West Bengal to be set up by the Calcutta Electric Supply Corporation will be funded by external credit totalling US $ 250 million. Of this, $ 100 million would come form the International Finance Corporation of the World Bank, $ 50 million from Asian Development Bank and an export credit of $ 100 million which will be backed by counter trade.

Another project to be financed by external credit is Bakreshwar, also in West Bengal. The project was to be financed with Soviet assistance, but since this is now uncertain, India is in search of external assistance, preferably from multilateral funding agencies.

Focus on Energy Efficiency

India could pioneer the exploration of energy efficiency opportunities on behalf of developing countries, even as it improves its own economic condition and industrial competitiveness, states the latest report of the International Institute of Energy Conservation.[3] The World Bank and the Asian Development Bank could be tapped for funds even though less than one per cent of the World Bank's energy loans to the country support end-use energy efficiency projects, according to the report prepared by the Washington-based organisation with regional office in Bangkok and Santiago.

The report was released under the title: "The least cost energy path for India: Energy efficient investment banks (MDBs) "The report specifies over a dozen major actions and policy efforts to promote cost-effective energy efficiency options. The report notes that considerable scope exists for energy savings in the country. The national transmission losses in electricity is about 23 per cent. With an installed capacity of nearly 70,000 megawatts (MW), the annual losses about to 17,000 MW. It costs approximatly Rs. 3 crore to install one megawatt capacity.

Studies have shown, that by transmitting electricity at 11 Kilovolt or 33 KV mode instead of the inefficient 440 volts. The capital investments required could be got back in four years. This is just an example.

There are nearly 400 sugar mills in the country, 200 of which are in the 500 tonnes crushing per day (TCD) category. Four hundred more will come up by the end of this decade. A mill generates about five megawatts of electricity which is fully consumed within. With minor modifications, a mill could produce 26 MW and provide nearly 15 MW surplus power to the sectors. This could be done easily. More efficient use of energy could reduce the growing cost of energy service and their environmental impacts, which have accompanied India's

3. *The Times of India*, November 22, 1991.

rapid industrial expansion. To meet the energy demands during the Eighth plan, the country would require nearly Rs. 234,000 crore of investment.

The World Bank and the International Monetary Fund have a major opportunity to contribute to the economic development of India. Investing in energy-efficiency will improve industrial productivity and limit unnecessary outflow of hard currency for expensive energy suply. The Banks need to integrate energy efficiency into all of their lending, not just to the energy sector, but also to the major energy-consuming sectors, such as industry, transportation and agriculture.

The study says the World Bank is the largest single foreign energy investor in India. From 1980 to 1990, the bank provided more than US $ 12.2 billion (Rs. 31,200 crore) for energy projects. About US $ 1.4 billion (12 percent) was provided at concessional rates. Between 1986 (the first year of ADB lending to India) and 1990, the ABD provided US $ 812 million for energy, all at non-concessional rate. Almost the most innovative energy-conservation programmes of the World Bank is a pending US $ 250 million industrial loan. If approved, it will be the first World Bank loan devoted solely to energy conservation, and the largest energy-conservation loan ever offered by multilateral development bank.

The report recommends that the Bank and ADB implement a system of "integrated least-cost energy planning" in what all energy investment options are assessed on the basis of cost. For India, such planning would apply to all economic sectors receiving loans.

World Bank Funding Withheld For NPTC

The World Bank (WB) expressed concern over the National Power Transmission Corporation's (NPTC) "lack of firm arrangement for funding of the capital budget and the potential delays in project implementation, for WB funded power transmission projects which the recently formed corporation has taken over from the National Thermal Power Corporation

(NTPC). Many an eye-brow has been raised questioningly over the tearing hurry with which the Union Minister for Energy has been transferring assets and personnel from the National Thermal Power Corporation to its offshoot, the National Power Transmission Corporation. This has led to allegations that scarce resources are being used to prop up yet another public sector white elephant.

A World Bank mission, comprising both World Bank and Asian Development Bank representatives, which evaluated the implications of the transfer of assets to NPTC from power generating entities like NTPC, NHPC and others, has in its report, recommended that strict conditions are imposed on at NPTC to ensure that it generates adequate internal resources before the bank releases funds for NPTC programme. After all, when the NPTC came into existence in October 1989, it had been at the behest of the present State Minister for Energy Mr. Rai. It seemed destined to be a non-starter from the very outset, dogged as it was by some controversy or the other. Yet the NPTC kept on gasping for breath, sustained by a token budget of Rs 5 crore.

Starting on July 12,1991, the deputy secretary of the department of power (DoP) issued directives to the chief executives of NTPC and NPTC to enter into an agreement for effecting the transfer of transmission assets and manpower through power of attorney. It pointed out that NPTC's revenue currently consists only of management fees collected from the power generating companies, which are "sufficient to cover cash operating expenses only". After examining NPTC's projected expansion programmes and its ability to generate resources to fund these ambitious plans, the mission has called on NPTC to either substantially increase its cash generation — in other words like in tariffs - or reduce its investment programme.

The ensuing events made for some pretty dramatic stuff, according to a report published in Sunday, December 29,1991-January 4,1992.

The transfer and absorption notice of 2,500 employees from NTPC to NPTC led to widespread protests from trade unions and officers' associations.

The NPTC management retaliated by obtaining caveats in various courts against unions and associations. This spurred the Corporate Executive Association of NTPC (CEAN) to file writ and stay petitions in the Delhi High Court. The list of allegations is quite long and the vicious court battle threatens to put off hold, any future proposition that NPTC has on the drawing board. According to R.N.Kaul, deputy manager, power systems and general secretary of CEAN, "on all other occasions where one public sector unit was split into two, the employees were offered options.

The national Airports Authority is one such an example. But the NTPC employees were transferred forcibly. "In the new organisation, we stand to lose on many acounts", Kaul then warns, "If the principle of offering options is violated, service conditions in the public sector will be entirely at the discretion of the government. Forcible transfer of personnel from one public sector unit to another will give unlimited powers to the management, bureaucracy and politicians."

Next, the Japanese banks, led by the Industrial Bank of Japan (IBJ) in an angry letter to the NTPC, expressed concern about the bifurcation and threatened to terminate all loans. It doubted the new organisation's capability of repaying the loan and was dismayed at not having been consulted. Worse was to follow. A damning report by the World Bank's assessment team expressed concern about the financial viability and operation. Given the abysmal collection record in the power sector, the World Bank has informed NPTC in no uncertain terms that it will not fund future NPTC programmes unless NPTC can guarantee that there will be full letter of credit coverage for all its clients with more than two months arrears. It also has insisted that NPTC's total level of accounts receivable should not exceed a return on equity of RBI rate plus 5 per cent. Further, the mission has pointed out that the yawning gap in funds outlay has not been filled by the Indian government so far and has insisted that both the Indian government and NPTC provide it with a properly approved funding plan for remainder of 1991-92 and 1992-93 in order to ensure that NPTC's ambitious transmission projects under consideration are implemented properly. The World Bank mission has criticised the government for not delaying the release of the promised funds to NPTC. It has noted that NPTC's proposed capital outlay for fiscal year 1991-92 was Rs 664 crore, of which Rs 262 crore had been up in September 30,1991 A further Rs 197 crore was to be provided by the owner of the assets and the balance Rs 205 crore by the government.

While the transfer from the generating units is hanging fire becuase of the court case, it has "expressed concern" over the fact that the government has released only Rs 3 crore so far and is evading giving a firm date to the bank for the release of an additional Rs 100 crore as equity funding in NPTC, scheduled to be released in fiscal 1992-93. Evaluating NPTC's projected financial health, the mission noted that, if the current tariff structure remained, NPTC's return on assets in operation would be 13 per cent, "which is negative in real terms." It feels that NPTC's projection of its own contribution to investment (self financing ratio) of 11 to 22 per cent per annum is by itself inadequate and even this level assumes considerable levels of government equity contributions and loan and bond mobilisation in the domestic as well as foreign markets, "whose feasibility is yet to be assessed."

So much for administrative jugglery. But technically as well, gaping holes are apparent in the bifurcation. For instance, the proposal to set up a central grid under NPTC. For this purpose, it sought to take over the transmission assets and power systems, personnel of the four national power generating units — NTPC, NEEPCO (North Eastern Electricity Power Corporation), NHPC (National Hydro Power Corporation) and the NC (Nuclear Corporation). By implication, this means that NPTC will have under its control, the entire transmission system business, including an extra high voltage AC transmission grid spread conutrywide to connect super-thermal stations with major load centres. The argument given by the power ministry is that a national grid would ensure optimum utilisation, minimise costs and enable inter-state need-based distribution. Sounds good. But facts speak otherwise.

The claim of seeking to build up a national grid rings hollow. The transmission segment of state sectors, which constitute 60 per cent of national transmission systems, fall beyond NPTC's purview. Moreover, under the Centre's open-door policy, when more private sector units will come into existence, the entire concept of a national grid would be rendered irrelevant. The bifuraction threatens to jeopardise the financial status of NTPC. Once assets worth Rs 5,000 crore are transferred from NTPC to NPTC under a power of attorney, NTPC looks to face a bleak financial future, making it yet another unviable public sector unit. Although for the time being they are clinging on to their assets, they could slip away at any moment. Out of NTPC's total profits of Rs 605 crore, transmission activities accounted for as much as Rs 140 crore. Coupled with this loss is a Rs 600 crore increase in debt services due to devaluation NTPC would clearly be in the red if the government insists on transferring their assets. NTPC has been asked to transfer all foreign financial assistance meant for transmission projects to NPTC. The tricky question is who will now bear the responsibility for repayment.

Set up in November, 1975 NTPC is the largest producer of electricity in the country with a commissioned capacity of 10335 MW and a transmission network of more than 16000 circuit Kms. Spearheading a dynamic drive to bring more power to the nation, NTPC has set five super thermal power stations — Singrauli, Korba, Ramagundam, Vindhyachal and Rihand and two gas based combined cycle power stations at Anta and Auraiya. At Farakka, stage I of three 200 MW units is completed and work is also progressing satisfactorily for setting up of two 500 MW units. Work is also progressing at Dadri for three more coal based units of 210 MW each apart from the unit which is now being synchronised. Work on Kahalgaon (coal), Talcher (coal), Kawas (Gas) and Dadri (Gas) are progressing as per schedule. In addition, the 720 MW Badarpur Thermal Power Station at New Delhi and the 270 MW BALCO captive power plant at Korba in Madhya Pradesh are also being managed by NTPC.

NTPC achieved a record generation of 46,879 million units during 1990-91 representing an increase of 14.64 per cent over last year and with 10.02 per cent return on capital employed, the Corporation's sales reached all time high of Rs 2,420 crore. It recorded an impressive profit of Rs 700.95 crore during 1990-91 as against the previous year's achievement of Rs 5,36.56 crore. With the total approved investment rising to Rs 18,624 crore, NTPC is now poised for further growth and consolidation to meet the energy requirements of the 21st century.

Within two years of its inception, the consultancy wing of NTPC has made a significant breakthrough in the international market by obtaining a contract for turnkey execution of 400 KV transmission lines from Dubai Electricity Company against stiff international competition. Assignments have been obtained from Hydroelectric Commission, Tasmania, the Damodar Valley Corporation, GVK industries, Orissa Power Generation Corporation among many others.

The World Bank had warned that it will not consider any requests from the National Thermal Power Corporation (NTPC) for new financing and in fact ongoing loan arrangements might "face repercussions" unless the thermal power giant improves its abysmal record of dues collection from its customers. A WB team, which recently explored a possible power systems project under separate loans to NTPC and NTPC, has, while passing strictures on NTPC's inability to contribute internal resources to its capital outlay plans, recommended the imposition of strict conditions which have to be met by the thermal power giant in order to obtain WB funding.

NTPC's bill collection, which averaged 77 per cent from June 1990 to June 1991, has, "despite NTPC's continuing efforts, deteriorated" the mission noted, mainly because of continuing poor collections from Bihar, Uttar Pradesh, DVC, West Bengal, Kerala and Himachal Pradesh. As of end of October, 1991, WB was concerned to note that NTPC's gross arrears had mounted to a staggering Rs 1580 crore, or 5.3 months sales equivalent. Current receivable at the same time, had mounted to Rs 1040 crore, equivalent to 3.5 months' sales.

Although NTPC has assured that current receivables would be brought down to below two months sales equivalent by January, 1992 and that negotiations with major defaulters are at an advanced stage for provision of adequate letter of credit (LC) coverage so that this position can be sustained, the Bank has expressed considerable scepticism over this claim and has asked NTPC to demonstrate factual improvement in the level of receivables. The bank has also stressed that a pre-condition for future funding will be the immediate implementation by all state governments of a minimum tariff of 50 paise/kilowatt hour on agriculture, is essential if the financial viability of state electricity boards is to be improved, which is the only way in which NTPC can improve its own collection position. Noting the huge gap between NTPC's projected investment plan, which amounts to US $ 6 billion, and its current resource position WB has asked NTPC and the Indian government to explore the possibilites of making a substantial share issue in order to raise resources for its investment programme.

NTPC TODAY

Plant	Location	Capacity (MW) Commissioned
Coal Based		
Singrauli	Sonebhadra (U.P.)	2000
Korba	Bilaspur (M.P.)	2100
Ramagundam	Karimnagar (A.P.)	2100
Farakka	Murshidabad (W.B.)	600
Rihand	Sonebhadra (U.P.)	1000
Vindhyachal	Sidhi (M.P.)	1260
Kahalgaon	Bhagalpur (Bihar)	—

Talcher	Dhenkanal (Orissa)	—
NCTPP	Ghaziabad (U.P.)	210
Gas Based		
Anta	Kota (Rajasthan)	1065
Auraiya	Etawah (U.P.)	1065
Kawas	Surat (Gujarat)	—
Dari	Ghaziabad (U.P.)	—
The Corporation also manages		
Badarpur	Delhi	720
Balco	Bilaspur (M.P.)	270

Source : The Times of India, December 21,1991.

Finally, the Prime Minister, Mr Narasimha Rao said the major part of the Eighth Plan investment would be in the infrastructural sector so that the country was able to take in new industries. Both the direction of economic reforms and the intention to implement them were there with the government from 1980 onwards. In fact, during Rajiv Gandhi's regime, a white paper on the public sector was prepared. He indicated that political considerations came in the way and there were bitter controversies. The paper did not see the light of the day and it was decided that it would be revived and executed later, on the assumption that Mr Gandhi would come back to power. "What we have started doing is exactly what we wanted to do, but the speed of economic reforms has been forced on us by the desperate situation we are in," he added.

Chapter VII

Energy Conservation

The rapid increase in the import bill for crude oil and petroleum products has been causing concern to all of us, according to B. Shankaranand, minister for petroleum & natural gas. Even a limited saving in the consumption of petroleum products by 10 per cent, through adoption of appropriate conservation measures, would result in a saving of more than Rs. 1000 crore. The potential for conservation, however, is much larger and all efforts need to be made to realise it to the extent possible. India's per capita consumption of energy is 200 kg of oil equivalent compared to World's average of 1540 kg. Oil continues to be the most important source of energy in India and India continues to be a net importer of oil.

Only 52 per cent of India's total crude oil requirements are met through indigenous production. In the year 1990-91 India spent about Rs. 10,000 crore for importing crude oil and petroleum products. India's demand for petroleum products is growing at a compound rate of about 7 per cent per annum. At this rate of growth, India would need about 100 million tonnes of petroleum products by the turn of this century.

The table shows changes in geographical distribution of hydrocarbon reserves.

	Thousand Million Tonnes 1984.	Thousand Million Tonnes 1990
Total North America	5.5	5.3
Total Latin America	11.7	17.1
Total Western Europe	3.3	1.9
Total USSR & E. Europe	11.4	8.1
Total West-Asian Region	54.2	89.5
Total Africa	7.5	7.9
Total Asia & Australia	2.5	6.7
Total World	96.1	136.5

Source : BJP Statistical Review of World Energy, June 1991 and June 1995.

In India, petroleum refineries are not only energy supplier but also large energy consumers. A typical refinery consumers about 6 to 10 per cent of the energy equivalent of the feed stock processed in various forms such as fuel, electrical power and steam depending upon the complexity, age of that particular refinery, the type of feed stocks, products and operating severity. Oil refineries all over the world started energy conservation programmes immediately after 1973 oil shock.

The growth rate of world oil consumption during the period 1950-1973 was of the order of 7.5 per cent per annum with the LDCs having a higher growth of 8.8 per cent as compared to 6.9 per cent for the industrialised nations. All this has changed with oil shocks in 1973 and later in 1979 as a result of which the developed countries were able to rapidly realign their oil consumption pattern by implementing programmes for more efficient use of oil and in certain cases, resort to substitution by other fuels. The present level of crude oil production from onshore/offshore indigenous sources is of the order of 33 million tonnes per annum as against the consumption level of petroleum products amounting to over 54.7 million tonnes per annum. As per current projections, the demand for petroleum products is expected to rise to over 100 million tonnes by the end of the decade, by which time the indigenous crude production may have increased to around 58 million tonnes, leaving an uncovered deficit of 49 million tonnes.

India is a net oil importer and during the last two decades, the oil import has increased substantially. From less than 9 per cent of foreign exchange earnings through commodity exports during the 1960s, the net oil import bill, following the first oil crisis, increased to over 75 per cent in 1980-81. This occured despite an increase in relative self-sufficiency in oil supplies from a mere 60 per cent in 1960-61 to over 30 per cent during the 1970s. Since 1980-81 the net oil import bill has seen a substantial reduction which has been largely due to a rapid increase in indigenous crude production as self-sufficiency in oil supplies increased to over 60 per cent by 1983-84, and weak oil prices in the international market.

On the other hand due to the Gulf Crisis the oil import bill rose considerably consequent upon the crude price hike (from US $ 18 to US $ 25 per barrel between July and October 1990). It was over Rs. 10,000 crore in 1990-91 and is expected to be around Rs. 13,000 crore during the financial year 1991-92.

The twin subjects of petroleum conservation and augmentation are two faces of the same coin each as important as the other to India, said N.Sankar, President, Associated Chambers of Commerce & Industry of India. Conservation should be achieved through a sector-wise approach. Consumers of petroleum products could be divided into four major categories, namely, transport, industry, domestic/household and agriculture. These are examples of several countries which have proved that conservation is an achievable task. Owing to energy conservation efforts, Japan's energy intensity, i.e. energy consumption per unit of GNP has improved by about 30 per cent from 1973 to 1985. For the industrial sector, as energy consumption accounts for more than 50 per cent of the total energy consumed in the country, the performance of the industrial sector in the area of energy conservation has great bearing on the total energy efficiency of Japan.

The efforts of energy intensive industries such as iron and steel, cement, pulp and paper, and fertilisers, is of great significance. In the case of iron and steel, the energy consumption rate was 78.8 per cent in 1985 compared to the 1973 level, which means a decrease of about 21 per cent. In the case of petrochemicals, a 32 per cent decrease was registered, cement has shown a 28 per cent improvement, and paper and pulp a 25 per cent improvement in energy use. These have been brought about in same cases, by better management of energy use with little or no investment, as in housekeeping measure, but in other cases by aggressive investment in energy efficient equipment. In petroleum and petroleum products at least 10 per cent saving in import can be brought about by avoiding wastage, increased use of oil efficient and fuel saving technologies.

Energy consumption in the industrial sector is roughly 60 per cent of commercial energy consumption, three times that of the transport sector and 30 times that of agriculture. India's high industrial energy intensity is due to several reasons. In the post- independence era, successive development plans have laid emphasis on building up a self-reliant industry and a strong infrastructure. With the result, a great deal of investment was made in developing basic industries such as steel, cement, aluminium, fetilisers, heavy chemicals, refineries, petro-chemicals, pulp and paper among others. These are inherently energy intensive. Most of the investment was made in the 1960's and early 1970's when energy was much cheaper than it is now and is consequently energy inefficient by today's standards.

Recent energy audit case studies of several countries have shown the tremendous potential of energy conservation. The table highlights this:

Company	Annual Savings Potential (Rs. Lakhs)	% of Energy Bill	Net Savings (Rs. Lakhs).	Estimated Investment	Payback period (Years)
A	44.0	15.0	6.0	63.0	1.44
B	51.0	16.0	14.0	48.0	0.9
C	291.0	9.0	19.0	207.0	0.7
D	287.0	41.0	54.0	707.0	2.5
E	380.0	30.0	7.7	349.5	1.0
F	672.0	40.0	18.5	768.2	1.5
G	2.0	16.0	0.38	3.32	1.6
H	8.48	16.0	0.47	9.23	1.2
I	26.23	16.3	7.56	14.46	0.5
J	4.53	27.0	1.0	7.54	1.6
K	0.64	11.5	0.41	0.45	1.0
L	0.86	17.0	0.11	0.73	1.0
M	9.23	10.0	1.15	9.23	1.0
N	365.0	16.0	80.0	100.0	1.0
O	17.74	23.0	8.28	17.67	1.0
P	345.97	17.0	52.82	244.62	1.0
Total	2505.68		271.38	2551.05	Less than 3 Years.

India's energy requirements are met from a variety of sources, both commercial and non-commercial, inspite of substantial increases during the last four decades, in the supply of commercial source of energy such as coal, oil & gas and electricity, non-commercial sources, dominated by fuel wood, still meet around half of our energy needs, particularly in the rural India. Besides, being inefficient in terms of end-use. Loss of fuelwood also results in adverse impact on the environment. There exists a substantial potential in non-conventional sources such as: solar, wind and tidal energy, etc. but we are still far away from making these sources cost effective.

How much energy does India need in the future? The most highly developed countries presently use 170 Kilowatt hours of energy of all kinds per day per capita mostly in the form of fossil fuels i.e. Coal, Oil and Gas. Assuming that we can get by with one third of this amount and that our population will stabilise at 100 crore during the next century, we would need to produce energy of all kinds at a rate of about 25 million megawatts as against 0.1 million MW today i.e. the availability of energy must be increased by 250 times. To comprehend this in physical terms, it is useful to be aware of the following energy equivalents:

1. Tonnes of oil: 1100 cu.m of gas
2. Tonnes of coal: 12 MW Hours of electricity

Recoverable reserves per capita

	Coal (Tonnes)	Oil (Tonnes)	Gas (w.m.)
RUSSIA	20066	30.3	142860
USA	13488	16.0	25000
CHINA	1168	2.3	900
INDIA	176	0.78	1005

On the question of self-sufficiency in crude oil, it should be noted that even the U.S.A. with an availability of 16.0 tonnes/capita is a major importer. India with a current availability of 0.78 tonnes/capita would need more to become self-sufficient, at some time in the future, a situation we should not realistically plan on. The gas and coal scenarios are not much better. It could appear that the energy scenario for India in the next century is a matter of great concern.

Reducing consumption of petroleum products through conservation efforts has received special attention in the last decade and energy intensity particularly the oil intensity has been brought down by developed economies by 30 to 35 per cent. Indian economy continues to be highly petroleum intensive. The oil intensity has in fact increased from 1.98 Kg/Rs. 100 of G.D.P in the 1970s to 2.72 kg/Rs. 100 of G.D.P. in the 1980s (calculated at 1980-81 prices). This brings to focus the enormous potential that exists for saving petroleum products can be saved through efficiency improvement and conservation efforts which calculated on current prices works out to about Rs. 6000 by 1994-95. The transport sector consumes about 40 per cent of the petroleum products followed by industry 25 per cent. Household 19 per cent, agriculture 9 per cent. The import bill for the current year 1991-92 is expected to be about Rs. 13,000 crore and diesel accounts for about 42 per cent.

Looking to the present petroleum scenario in the country it is seen the transport sector consumed around 54.05 MMTs, in 1989-90, whereas the consumption during 1990-91 was around 54.87 MMTs, registering a marginal increase. The consumption of fuels with transport sector including ATF during 1989-90 was 26.83 MMTs and in 1990-91 it was 26.89 MMTs. Internal circumstances, there should have been at least 6 per cent to 8 per cent growth in transportation fuel demand due to dependence on road transport sector and increased in diesel vehicle population thereof. However, during the time, the demand was contained.

The demand of petroleum products is expected to touch around 98 MMTs (Ref. 8th Plan Demand Estimates) in 2000 A.D., whereas the indigenous availability would be limited to around 58 MMTs which would leave a deficit of over 40 MMTs which has to be inevitably met by imports at the then escalated world oil price which could be any where in the order of $ 40 to $ 60 per barrel. The transportations fuel demand during this corresponding period would be around 48 MMTs whereas the actual availability may be limited to around 50 to 60 per cent of the actual demand.

During the eighties, the transport sector witnessed a number of fuel efficient petrol driven vehicles coming to the market, particularly Maruti, Premier 118 NE and Contessa Classic (with 1SUZU engine). Further there was a boom in two wheeler population which now accounts for 60 per cent of MS consumption in the country. If oil consumption in the road transport sector is to be slashed effectively, a comprehensive plan has to be implemented to promote efficient mass transport and rapid transit systems in major cities, on the aviation front the conventional aircraft viz. DC-3s, Caravells, Boeing 707s have been phased out and replaced by more efficient Boeing 737s/747s, and Air Bus 300/320. Besides over the years due to improved/advanced operation and maintenance practices, continuous monitoring of fuel uplifts/consumption, celibration of refueller delivery meters, the consumption of ATF has been reduced appreciably.

Annual production of coal in late sixties and early seventies was around 70 million tonnes. The oil crisis of early seventies led to recognise the importance of coal as primary source of energy in national economy. High demand of coal led mining engineers to plan a switch over from conventional type of underground methods of opencast mining methods deploying HEMM, Shovel-dumper combination system became popular because of its flexibility, great mobility and scope for change in size and capacity with variation in demand. There has been lot of attempts to make this system more efficient reducing on the cost of oil energy through efficient utilisation of HEMM and development of alternative mechanical design. It has been observed by A.A. Niazi, Chairman, IBP Co. Ltd. that simple follow up on preventive maintenance and proper design of haul roads could result in saving of oil to the tune of 9-15 per cent. Dump trucks have been identified an area whose the maximum fuel oil is consumed.

Process industry primarily uses energy for process heating and for generation of utilities including electric power and steam. Hydrocarbons are also used as the feedstock. Improvements in the use of energy therefore can come about directly through employing more efficient processes which will permit lower consumption of energies and alternatively through the addition, modification or improvements in existing plant and equipment. In a study carried out in the USA it has been found that more than 50 per cent of the total energy wasted to environment could be saved by introducing energy conservation measures on the heat transfer equipment themeselves. While 30 per cent improvement could be possible by looking after the process equipment such as fired heaters, heat exchangers and distillation columns which are the major energy guzzlers; the balance 20 per cent saving could be possible as a result of the systematic energy audit and optimisation study.

Since its commisioning in 1955, Bharat Petroleum Refinery located in Bombay was designed to process 2.20 million metric tonnes per annum (MMT/PA). In 1985, a major expansion scheme for Debottle necking of crude Distiller and Instillation of Additonal Secondary Processing Facilities was completed. This project enabled processing of any combination of Bombay High and West Asian crudes at a sustained capacity of 6 MMT PA. This versatile Refinery has so far processed 41 different types of crude including 5 indigenous crudes (i.e. Ankleshwar, Bombay High, Ratha, Heera and Panna.

BPCL has invested about Rs. 153 crore so far on Energy Conservation and pollution Abortment measures resulting in savings of Rs. 28 crore per annum. BPCL has put up proposals under the 8th plan period in these areas which envisage a further savings of 19.788 MT/annum of fuel equipment to a foreign exchange of Rs. 9.6 crore per annum when commissioned. There has been a progressive reduction in the energy consumption at the refinery by the implementation of the measures mentioned and the fuel saving achieved has increased from 1700 MT/A. in the year 1985-86 to 127.722 MT/A in 1990-91 resulting in a foreign savings of Rs. 20.4 crore per annum in 1990-91. The energy consumption in terms of MBTU/BBL/NRG factor has been significantly improved from

189.2 in 1985-86 to 139.2 in 1990-91 amounting to a reduction of 26 per cent in the last five years.

Annual consumption of lubricants in the country is currently of the order of 0.9 million tonnes, which in terms of equivalent lube base oil at international prices would be valued at about Rs. 850 crore. Considering the current domestic prices of finished lubricants, the actual size of the lubricant market would be about three times this figure. Lubricating greases consituties 5 to 6 per cent of the total lubricants market and speciality industrial lubricants such as metal working oils just preventives, rolling oils, etc. would account for another 9 to 10 per cent. Lubricanting grease and petroleum specialists would thus account for over Rs. 125 crore worth of lube base oils at international prices.

It is believed that potential exists for reducing the specific consumption of this group of products in terms of mineral oils by 10 to 30 per cent. In one steel plant, the rolling lubricant consumption averaged around 1.8 litres per tonne of steel rolled. With this now lubricant having a mineral oil content of less than 50 per cent as against 80 per cent in earliest generation rolling oils, the specific consumption of rolling lubircant has been reduced to about 1.2 litres per tonne of steel.

The sprayble greases were being entirely imported and imports had reached a level of about Rs. 2 crore (CIF value) by 1990. Balmer Lawrie took up a project to develop indigenous substitues in close cooperation with some of the cement plants and cement machinery manufacturers. The conventional (greases used in roller bearings of Rail Wagons and Coaches were found to work satisfaction by only for 18 to 36 months against the expected minimum service life of 54 months. Passanger cars, buses and commercial vehicles in our country have been traditionally using sodium based wheel bearing greases, which offer service life of about 15,000 kilometres. Similar benefits of oil conservation, cost reduction and technological upgradation, can be brought about in many other areas as well.

Of the various types of lubricants, engine crankcase oil consititute the single largest group — accounting for over 70 per cent of all lubricants. Annual consumption of engine crankcase oils in India is presently over 500,000 MT. These are used in internal combustion engines used for such diverse applications as passenger cars, buses, commercial vehicles, tractors railroad and marine engines, stationary generator sets, scooter, and motor cycle, heavy earth moving machinery, small agricultural pump sets, etc.

Until recently, drain intervals (oil charge periods) as engine lubricants varied from around 5,000 KMs in passenger cars tc 9,000 KMs in commercial diesel vehicle. Through sustained efforts of the oil industry and the OEMs assisted by additive companies, it has been possible to develop imposed lubricant formulations to increase the lubricant life viz, drain intervals to 10,000 and 18,000 KMs respectively. This has resulted in substantial savings not only to the users themselves, but also to the national economy in terms of oil conservation. Currently lube base stocks used to formulate engine oils, are being imported to the extent of 40 per cent of the country's demand, engine oil conservation is therefore of prime importance.

India has vast reserves of natural gas estimated at over 100 billion cubic metres. Of this a large portion (valued at Rs. 2,000 crore) is not being flared owing to lack of facilities available for compression and transportation to contain such wastage. This area ought to be given an urgent attention. The estimate of energy based upon planned rate of growth of economy indicates that requirement of petroleum would increase from present consumption level of 54 million tonnes to 100 million tonnes by 2000 A.D. The present level of demand satisfaction of oil is about 66 per cent. However as demand strips indigenous availability the long terms project crude oil production, the demand satisfaction level may decline to about 63 per cent.

The recent trend of oil and gas find in the country indicate that future discoveries are likely to be more in the form of Natural Gas. The availability of natural gas presently is 17 million tonnes of oil equivalent and long term projections based on geological estimates indicate that gas availability will increase to 30 million tonnes of oil equivalent by the year 2000.

Natural Gas can easily be used in place of liquid of solid energy sources as fuel and feedstock. Use of Natural Gas in the various sectors is summarised below.

Sector	
Feedstock	
'Fertilizer'	Naphtha, Fuel Oil, Coal
"Chemical"	Naphtha
Energy	
'Industrial	Fuel oil, Diesel, Coal
'Commercial/Domestic	LPG, Kerosene, Diesel, Coal
Power	
'Captive	Diesel
'Peak & Base Load	Diesel, Coal, Fuel Oil.

Natural Gas application in fertilizer plant results into saving of around 15% capital cost and 5% power energy consumption as compared to naphtha based plants. In case of Petrochemicals also, it gives higher Clefine yields (85% against 55% for naphtha based plant). Use of gas in power generation in combined cycle and also in local generations is going to contribute significantly in reduction of use of diesel run power plant/captive power set. As fuel, natural gas has significant advantage in terms of ease of operation and total control and regulation of combustion. It provides greater flexibility and opportunity to improve the efficiency. The concept of cogeneration in natural gas increases the efficiency of utilisation in the range of 80-90 per cent. Thus, system is not only as energy conservation system but also improves the economies of the consumers.

Natural gas provides better opportunity to recover sensible heat upto 60 degree C from the products of combustion. With proper provisioning of an appropriate heat recovery system the efficiency can increase by 15 per cent.

The natural gas is a premium source of energy for domestic and commercial sector, where the user is benefited from assured uninterrupted supply and the environmental compatibility and is more economical option as compared to the use of LPG.

Natural gas does not only provide the option of replacing liquid petroleum in various sectors but offers great potential of conservation of energy in these applications due to its inherent properties and also on account of updated technology and equipment available for utilisation on natural gas for achieving higher efficiency.

Dhruv M. Sawhney, President, CII elaborated the causes for energy inefficiency in industry.[1]

Industry managers are unaware of the potential for energy efficiency and its profitability. This lack of awareness is particularly pervasive in industries where the energy share of production cost is relatively low and correspondingly energy efficiency is not critical to performance and to competitiveness.

Even when the awareness gap is closed, there often remains a sizeable expertise gap. Undertaking an energy efficiency programme of ten requires a degree of expertise, that industry managers, particularly in industries where energy represents a relatively low share of the total cost, often do not possess. such expertise gap may often be filled by so called energy service companies which take up the entire job on a project basis. such companies are only now emerging in India.

Technology gap:

Closing the technological gap requires continuing research and development activity. R & D activities in the energy area have supported research in the area of renewable sources such as biogas, solar and wind power, and are typically geared towards rural application. Very little R & D has been carried out in the area of energy use in the industry. It is necessary to

1. The Sunday Times of India, February 16, 1992.

allocate some resources to industrial R & D base, the better is the ability to acquire technology from abroad.

Lack of effective General Co-ordination: Central Government's policy, indulging the coordination of desirable actions and incentives has a major impact on energy efficiency performance. Until recently the government's efforts in this area have been fragmented.

Lack of knowledge base: For the Central planning body to articulate and then coordinate the implementation of an appropriate strategy to correct the problem, requires an adequate knowledge base. It is necessary to know on a fairly disaggreagated basis, the patterns of energy usage and the potential for improvement, industry by industry, as well as the costs of achieving such improvement. The present knowledge gap in this respect needs to be closed. The central authorities do not at the present moment have sufficiently disaggregated data on energy usage to formulate industry specific improvement strategies.

Obsolete Equipment: Improved energy efficiency requires attention to physical plant and equipment facilities. Much of the energy intensive industries were established in the 1960's and the early 1970's before energy efficient technologies became as important as they are now. As a result, there exists a potential for energy savings especially in the steel, cement, and fertilizer sectors, were the basic technologies applied need to be upgraded if greater levels of energy efficiency are to be achieved. This requires a sizeable investment. Housekeeping measures usually have a very high rate of return, since little investment is involved. Where the basic technology employed is uptodate, retrofitting to improve energy efficiency can usually secure high return as well.

National Strategy

Identify a central co-ordinating body which would:

—Minor performance

—determine national priorities for improving energy efficiency.

—advise government on appropriate policies and strategies to boost demand for energy savings investment and to strengthen the needed supply response.

—co-ordinate the implementation of agreed strategies.

To strengthen the existing knowledge base, the central co-ordinating cell would have to: Commission and support sub sector studies to establish and define targets for energy consumption by sub sector.

—establish and retain a comprehensive database on national industrial energy usage.

The following measures would need to be evaluated for their efficacy and feasibility:

—Tax excessive consumption and consumption of dirty fuels. Impose penalty surcharges on industries consuming energy at levels of specific consumption in excess of established norms.

Give incentives or tax relief to energy saving and pollution abating investment.

Eliminate in a phased manner, consistent with broader trade reform proposals for the capital goods sector, indirect taxes (tariffs, excise and sales tax) on energy savings/pollution abating devices and equipment.

Give relief on direct taxes by permitting a deduction based on the extent to which specific energy consumption/pollution discharge is less established norms for each industry.

To improve the technological state of the art, it is necessary to undertake R & D activity. A program for providing subsidy of R & D activity undertaken either by publicly funded research institutes or private sector enterprises should be formulated. In the area of energy efficiency, it is necessary to focus R & D effort on problems with potentially high pay-off and high chance of success — a priority setting exercise.

Strengthened institutional support measures required would include:

—establish demonstration centres

—establish award and competition schemes

—establish energy efficiency standards for industrial equipment and household appliances.

—strengthen training efforts at all levels — senior management, engineers, technicians and consultants.

—develop and administer in R&D programme based on established priorities.

—change performance criteria for SEB's.

—encourage SEB's to purchase power at economic rates from cogeneration plants established by industry.

Energy efficiency improvement in industry would require undertaking of investment projects within industry itself. There are two sub sectors in this:

(a) those in which energy constitutes such a large share of project cost that management actively seeks ways of reducing energy costs and energy consumption indicators are routinely used as measures of plant performance.

(b) those where energy constitutes a relatively low share of product cost and management assigns low priority to optimizing energy use.

For category (a) industries, the prime motivation may be found in relative prices, pricing policies and the competitive imperatives. Further, the encouragement of demonstration projects — projects undertaken by one firm in an industry that may serve to spur others to undertake similar projects--may be a useful way of encouraging energy efficiency projects.

One of the major factors responsible for the rapid increase in Energy Demand is the distorted pricing structure. Existing energy prices do not reflect the true cost of supplying energy to the consumers nor do they take into account the cross-price effects on demands for substitute fuels.

Subisdies have become a way of life in this country and cannot be wished away overnight. It must be ensured that subsidies are minimised gradually and that most of it reaches the targeted consumer segments. There is no incentive to the consumers to conserve energy. The Tariff structure should be conducive to energy conservation and at the same time not penalise the poorer segments.

CII Initiatives

The CII National Committee on Energy under the Chairmanship of Mr. Rajive Kaul set up Task Forces to deliberate upon issues related to:

—Power

—Oil & Gas

—Non-conventional Energy Sources

—Co-generation

The Task Force on Non-conventional Energy Sources met under the Chairmanship of Dr. N.D.Joshi and decided to bring out a status report.

CII in co-operation with the Dept. of Power and World Bank organised an International Conference on Co-generation. One of the important recommendations of the Conference was formation of a Task Force on Co-generation. CII and CEA have set up the Task Force which is working on bringing out the potential of co-generation in various industry sectors.

CII-EEC organised ENCON '91 to specifically focus on Energy Conservation and Energy Management Technologies and Equipment. As a part of ENCON '91 Technology Co-operation Seminars/Conferences were held.

CII with NIFES, UK and EEC are conducting a study on Measuring Instruments for Energy Audits. The objective of the study is to assess the opportunities and barriers in India for joint ventures between European manufacturers and Indian counterparts for manufacture of Energy measuring Instrument in India.

CII alongwith Karnataka State Electricity Board and ABB Ltd. conducted a System study on Reactive Power Compensation for Karnataka State Electricity Board's Transmission & Distribution system for improving voltage profile & reducing T & D losses. Papers published on energy:

—Status paper on Co-generation

—Status paper on Energy Policies

—Electricity Tariff policy: Need for a new look

CII is the Lead Agency in the Southern region for the UNDP- EMC Energy Bus Project.

Note:

Tonnes Oil Equivalent (TOE)–a measure which allows the aggregation of different energy sources viz coal, oil, gas, hydropower, nuclear power (primary sources) and coke, petroleum products, thermal power (secondary power).

Appendix

Hot Fushion Experiment: A New Energy Source[1]

The success of a hot fusion experiment using tritium in addition to deuterium in magnetic confinement reported by the European collaborative project. Joint European Torus (JET) the world's largest fusion device, in Britain represents only one further step towards the development of a new source of energy.

After the sage of discredited reports of cold fusion development, readers may be sceptical of what may be described as the "headline rate of scientific development".

In the nuclear fusion process, energy is produced when light atoms such as hydrogen are fused together to form helium. This is the process taking place continuously in the sun and stars, but to make it happen on earth, the equipment has to have fuel that is hotter than the central sun. This, of course, requires very stringent conditions but then there is the promise of the availability of unlimited and clear power based on plentiful fuel.

More than 10 years ago, this reporter asked an eminent researcher in controlled fusion reactions what would he do if given an unlimited amount of money on the condition that hydrogen power must be delivered by the end of the century. "I will transfer the amount to a numbered Swiss bank account", he said. Today, I asked a similar question to Dr. Paul Henri Rebut, director of the joint European Torus (JET) programme, who chose to tackle it seriously.

"We need two steps of 25 years each to reach the stage of commercial generation of power from this source," he said.

And from his remarks about the funding of fusion research it was obvious that he and his colleagues would require the

---

1. *The Times of India*, November 12,1991 (A step closer to New Energy Source by L.K. Sharma.

next 20 years to battle with politicians who do not think in terms of 50 years but in those of the next election.

Dr.Rebut said the next 25 years would be required for the operation of the next experimental reactor and the subsequent 25 would be needed for a demonstration model and whether or not this energy was then economically competitive would depend on several factors including the environmental laws obtaining at that time.

Thus even though the scientists at Calham laboratory near Oxford do desrve congratulations, it is clearly not yet time for the world communtiy to celebrate. What they have achieved through this preliminary is to demonstrate the scientific feasibility of the project. "Now the performance has to be improved by a factor of five".

Follow-up studies have begun and the equipment is to be shut down for maintenance for several months. Fresh experiments will be resumed, hopefully in an atomsphere of greater financial security, after the European governments have decided on the fate of the project after 1992. In the experiments that would follow the proportion of tritium to deuterium will be increased. In the one just completed, only 0.5 gram of tritium was used.

Dr. Rebut is going for a meeting in Moscow this week which will consider a more ambitious project, the international reactor (ITER). This will involve besides Europe, the US, Japan and the Soviet Union. If for some reason this grander project fails to materialise, Europe has its own plan for a bigger experimental reactor called NET which will be twice the linear dimensions of JET. Its construction could begin in 1997, provided funds running into millions of pounds are sanctioned.

NET will address the problems associated with obtaining a fully ignited, self-sustaining plasma to form the core of a fusion reactor and the technological and engineering aspects of incorporating super-conducting magnet coils, a tritium- breeding blanket module and that of sustaining hour-long pulses with thermal power output of around 1000 mw.

This is all about the future. In the experiment reported successful, the deuterium and tritium gas was heated to temperatures of around 200 million C—nearly more than 10 times hotter than the temperature in the centre of the sun. The peak fusion power generated reached almost 2 mw in a pulse lasting for two seconds and giving a total energy release equivalent to a megawatt for two seconds. At lower power in deuterium JET has already maintained stable conditions in the apparatus for periods up to one minute.

Magnetic Insulation:

When the JET scientists say the performance has to be improved by a factor of five, it covers numerical values relating to plasma temperature, energy confinement time and central density in plasma. Fusion reactions occur at a sufficient rate only at very high temperatures. Over 100 million C is needed for deuterium-tritum reaction whilst other reactions require even higher temperatures. The hot plasma must be well isolated away from material surfaces in order to avoid cooling the plasma (impurities) that would contaminate and further cool the plasma. In the Takamak system, the plasma is isolated by magnetic fields.

The efficiency of the magnetic insulation is measured by a quantity called the energy confinement time. This is the characteristic time-scale for plasma cooling when the source of heat is removed. The density of fuel ions must be sufficiently large for fusion reactions to take place at the requried rate. The fusion power generated is reduced if the fuel is diluted by impurity atoms released from surrounding material surfaces or by the accumulation of helium "ash" from the fusion reaction. As fuel ions are burnt in the fusion process they must be replaced by new fuel and the helim ash must be removed.

At such temperatures, the gas has become a plasma which can be contained by magnetic field. However, the challenge involved on doing this was best described by the father of the hydrogen bomb (uncontrolled fusion) Dr. Edward Teller who said it was like trying "to confine a jelly with rubber bands". Most of the fusion energy from this reaction appears as high-speed neutrons, which deposit their energy in a surrounding "blanket" of the reactor, heating it to several degrees celsius.

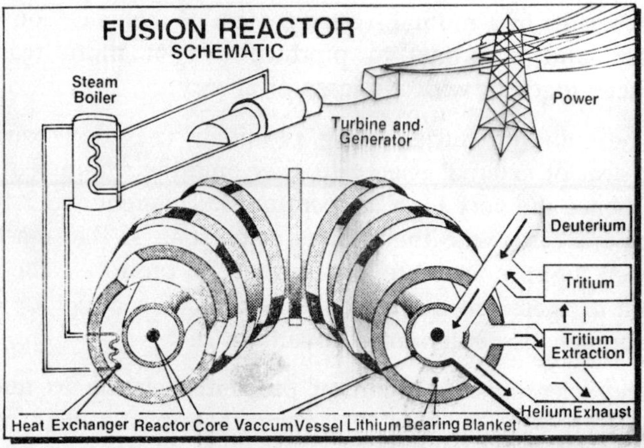

What is Nuclear Fusion?[2]

Last Saturday's breakthrough by a team of European scientists to produce controlled nuclear fusion for the first time, is a landmark achievement.

As reported, the generation of nearly two MW of power by the fusion of tritium and deuterium particles in the dough-nut- shaped reactor, was achieved at temperatures 20 times hotter than in the core of the sun.

This report came soon after the discovery of "cold fusion" led to shortlived dreams of cheap and unlimited power generation. The cold fusion theory soon became controversial and is now largely discredited.

---

2. *The Times of India,* November 12, 1991. Compiled by Ramesh Sharma.

Nuclear fusion is the energy-producing process that takes place continuously in the sun and the stars. The phenomenon occurs with two or more relatively light atomic nuclear coming together to form a heavier nucleus, releasing energy.

Fusion Reaction:

In a nuclear fusion reaction the close collision of two nuclei results in a mutual rearrangement of their nucleous (i.e. protons and neutrons) to produce two or more reaction products, together with a release of energy.

The colliding nuclei, being positively charged, require a great deal of external energy to overcome their mutual repulsion (hence the very high temperatures). This required relative energy increases with the number of protons, so that reactions between light nuclei are the easiest to produce. The best known of these are the reactions between the heavy isotopes of hydrogen — deuterium and tritium.

The scientific and technical problems relating to nuclear fusion have been the subject of research since the 1930s, when nuclear fusion was first discovered.

In 1939, the US physicist, Hans A. Bethe proposed that most of the energy of stars, including that of the sun, is derived from fusion reactions that proceed at very high temperatures and great densities. This hypothesis has become almost universally accepted.

Hydrogen Bomb:

Soon after World war II, efforts were made to create a weapon that would have tremendous power by utilising fusion reaction in a mixture of deuterium and tritium (the heavy isotopes of hydrogen), and in 1952-53 the so-called hydrogen bomb became a reality. The A-bombs dropped on Hiroshima and Nagasaki were fusion devices.

Interest in controlled nuclear fusion arises from the expectation that it may someday be used to produce cheap and plentiful power.

Since a primary fusion fuel, deuterium, occurs in sea water and is therefore obtainable in virtually inexhaustable supply by separating heavy hydrogen from water, (one atom of deuterium occurring per 5,000 atoms of hydrogen), solution of the fusion power problem would permanently solve the impending crisis due to rapid depletion of fossil fuels.

As a power source, the lack of radioactive waste products from the fusion reaction is another advantage. Also, a fusion reactor, by its very nature, can never explode - at worst it will collapse.

Caution of Fusion[3]

The 14-member Torus European team has made a significant breakthrough in creating power by nuclear fusion for the first time and should put paid to the dubious claims about a cold experiment conducted by scientists at Utah two years ago. Unlike the controversial joint US-British endeavour at Utah, the European scientists produced a megawatt of power by simulating the energy-creating capabilities of the sun, complete with extreme heat and collision techniques. By replicating what the sun and stars do, scientists hope to unleash the almost infinite capacity of the universe to combine the nuclear of heavy hydrogen isotopes to produce new atoms, giving off prodigious amounts of energy in the process. The experiment in Oxfordshire, however, is but a small though remarkable step towards copying what nature achieves continuously. The commercial production of power through remarkable step towards copying what nature achieves continuously. The commercial production of power through nuclear fusion will take at least half a century, as the team itself admits, and the cost per unit of power is expected to be prohibitive. However, it holds out tremendous hope for discovering a source of energy when conventional sources — mainly fisc fossil fuels, like coal and oil—are fast getting depleted. The competitor to Torus is the Tokamak reactor at Princeton University. A full-fledged fusion

---

3. The Times of India, November 12, 1991. (Editorial)

reactor is supposed to be at Princeton University. A full-fledged fusion rector is situated to produce about 1,000 tonnes of hydrogen a day, equivalent to 20,000 barrels of oil. Unlike fossil fuels, however, this power does not pollute. Its waste is also much less radioactive than that of conventional fusion power stations.

Where does the fusion success leave India? Some work on it has been going on at the Bhabha Atomic Research Centre and Tata Institute of Fundamental Research in Bombay, together with the Saha Institute of Nuclear Physics in Calcutta and a few other centres. The work is necessarily theoretical, considering that the cost of even an experimental fusion reactor is beyond the reach of some European countries, with a current tag of $ 5 billion. This once again raises the issue of the role of Indian science in general and nuclear research in particular. Should the country try and keep itself abreast of trends in the west by simulating such experiments, on however modest a scale? Or should it leave to the major powers to make such breakthroughs and hope to buy the technology when it is on the market? At a time when the entire economy is abandoning the precept of indigenisation and self-reliance, this issue gets even more sharply focussed and should confront the nuclear establishment in the next few years.

INDEX